MARRY TWO, THREE OR FOUR, BUT...

Navigating Polygamy And Its Untold Truths

BY: FAZAL CAREEM

Disclaimer:

The information presented in this book is based on the author's personal experiences and opinions. It is intended for educational and informational purposes only. The author and publisher make no warranties or representations regarding the accuracy or completeness of the content. Readers are encouraged to seek professional advice and conduct their own research regarding the subject matter.

CONTENTS

Author's Preface
& Acknowledgements

In the name of Allah, Most Beneficent, Most Merciful. Salutations and Peace be upon the Prophet Muhammed.

Around the end of 2023, when I was expecting certain changes in my life to happen, I began thinking about writing somewhat of a memoir around the subject of polygamy. Having had extensive experience being married to multiple wives at the same time, my aim was to use this experience to detail how best to navigate a very complex lifestyle. Hopefully, what is contained in the pages of this book will benefit those who may find themselves thinking about embarking on this journey by exploring what could very probably be in store for those brave souls – some may contend crazy - in their pursuit of more than one wife. When they are able to understand what could probably be in front of them, they will be better prepared to deal with the complexities that this lifestyle comes with. This applies to both men and women.

This book could not have been completed without the collaboration of several people, and I would like to acknowledge some of them for their contributions.

Firstly, my publishers, who gave me a lot of encouragement and guidance in this first-time effort of authorship. I look forward to continuing our working relationship for many years to come.

Secondly, I would like to thank my brother, who went through the initial draft and offered excellent advice and editing suggestions, which I believe significantly enhanced the quality of the writing. I wish he had done it quicker, but I forgive him for that.

I would also like to thank those men and women who read the early manuscript and provided excellent feedback, encouragement and kind words about my effort in writing this book. You know who you are.

This book would not be in existence without all the women I was blessed to have been married to. For some, our connection may have been severed, but the memories will stay forever.

My parents, who instilled in me the importance of respecting people and cultures different from mine.

To my children, who tolerated and continue to tolerate their dad in his endeavours and never make a fuss or make him feel ostracized, I love you to bits. You guys are my life and best friends!

Finally, to my first wife. The most beautiful and purest soul that I have ever met. I thank Allah for you. The appreciation I have for the sacrifices you have made to accommodate my desires cannot be put into words because I personally do not have the vocabulary to express them. You are the love of my life!

Fazal Careem

Introduction

The title of this book, "Marry Two, Three or Four But...?" for those who are unaware, is an extract of a verse found in the sacred scripture of the Muslims, The Qur'an, which allows Muslim men to marry more than one woman up to four at any one time.

But ...WHAT? – I hear you asking.

Read the book and stay the course to discover a lifestyle that many find contemptible while others find intriguing and even mysterious. I hope it will be an enlightening experience as well as an enjoyable and entertaining read for all of you, even for those who find it contentious. For now, I promise you a fascinating and enthralling encounter without a dull moment about what many consider a very emotive and controversial subject. Whether you are a protagonist or an antagonist, you will come to know things after reading the book that you did not know before. Fasten your seatbelt for a ride like no other!

A ride that will challenge the very foundations of what you thought you knew or did not know about marriage and women or wives - including those within your own lives - and, indeed, unearthing aspects of your own self hidden within the depths of your soul. You will confront and perhaps challenge long-held norms, viewing them with new lenses. Where stereotypes will be examined and questioned, and political in-correctness will be explored without censor. A ride of raw authenticity and unfiltered expressions that could also lead me on a collision course with angry and disgruntled critics charging me with misogyny, selfishness, and perhaps even perversion. That is a bridge to cross when and if it happens.

Before embarking on this ride with you, let me do two things. Firstly, I wish to define two words. "Polygamy" and "Polygyny." *Linguistically, Polygamy refers to any person (male or female) being married to two or more people at the same time. Polygyny, however, refers specifically to a man being married to two or more women.* For the purposes of this book, I will be using the word polygamy and its derivatives to describe a man marrying more than one woman, as this is the common usage among the masses. I will be exploring the practice of polygamy and what motivates men to engage in it, what emotions they experience during the journey, and how best they can navigate it while also taking into consideration the emotions of all those close to him who are affected by such a pursuit. My book will focus primarily on scenarios dealing with men wishing to marry a second wife **for the first time**, as opposed to when they want to include a third or fourth. The initial hurdles and intensities start with the pursuit of his second wife, and by the time he wishes to extend that list (if indeed he has what it takes), he would be a seasoned campaigner for this extremely peculiar and intriguing lifestyle. There are, of course, challenges in adding three and/or four into the mix but that is a discussion for another time, In Sha Allah. I will pay particular and close attention to the all-important first wife and ways to navigate her feelings and approach her at different junctures of a very emotional journey that she did not ask to take. And of equal importance are the sentiments of the lady who has agreed to be his second wife. She may be "second" chronologically, but with blood running through her veins and emotions permeating her soul, her feelings can never be relegated to second.

Let me also clarify what this book isn't about. While I began with a religious acknowledgment, it's important to emphasize that this isn't a religious text. I'm not here to justify any specific religious stance on polygamy; there are already plenty of books on that subject. Any religious references you encounter here are simply to provide context and ensure clarity.

That being said, this book isn't exclusively for Muslims. Polygamy is nearly extinct in Western and Eastern cultures, so discussing it from a modern perspective might evoke mixed feelings. Yet, infidelity persists, causing harm to families and communities worldwide. While some communities, like the Mormons, openly practice polygamy, I hope this book can bridge those gaps.

To first wives, Muslim women in particular, I did not forget and will not overlook the difficult and epically inconvenient transition that you will have to make to accommodate your husbands' desires. I have dedicated significant portions of this book recognising your feelings, emotions, and struggles while giving your husbands genuine advice (and sometimes a telling-off) in understanding exactly what kind of sacrifice you are making for him. Something he simply cannot afford to ignore while he pursues his desires.

To Muslim men, your emotions and struggles aren't dismissed either. I hope this book will challenge your perspective, showing that it's not just about fulfilling your desires but also about finding a sensible alternative to illicit affairs that benefits both you and society.

I understand that describing polygamy as "sensible" with "benefit" may raise some eyebrows and recognize that this claim may take me down a deep rabbit hole with my antagonists. Convincing them that the moon was made of green cheese would probably be easier. Regardless, I stand by my claim and explain the rationale in this book. Once you have read it, I am quite confident that most of you will agree. As for the sceptics, I would appeal to you to take a step back, understand the premises that I have articulated, and challenge and critique them if you wish, but be nice. Ultimately, we can agree to disagree and still be friends -- I hope.

This book's premise is rooted in historical norms about heterosexual relationships, acknowledging that exceptions exist. However, it is societal norms that usually shape customs, laws, and rules.

I've aimed for a light, engaging and upbeat tone throughout this book, sprinkled with anecdotes and humour, while recognizing that the pursuit of polygamy is also a serious matter for families to contend with. But I understand that not everyone will see eye to eye with me, and that's okay—it's all part of the discussion.

So, having said that, let's take this ride.

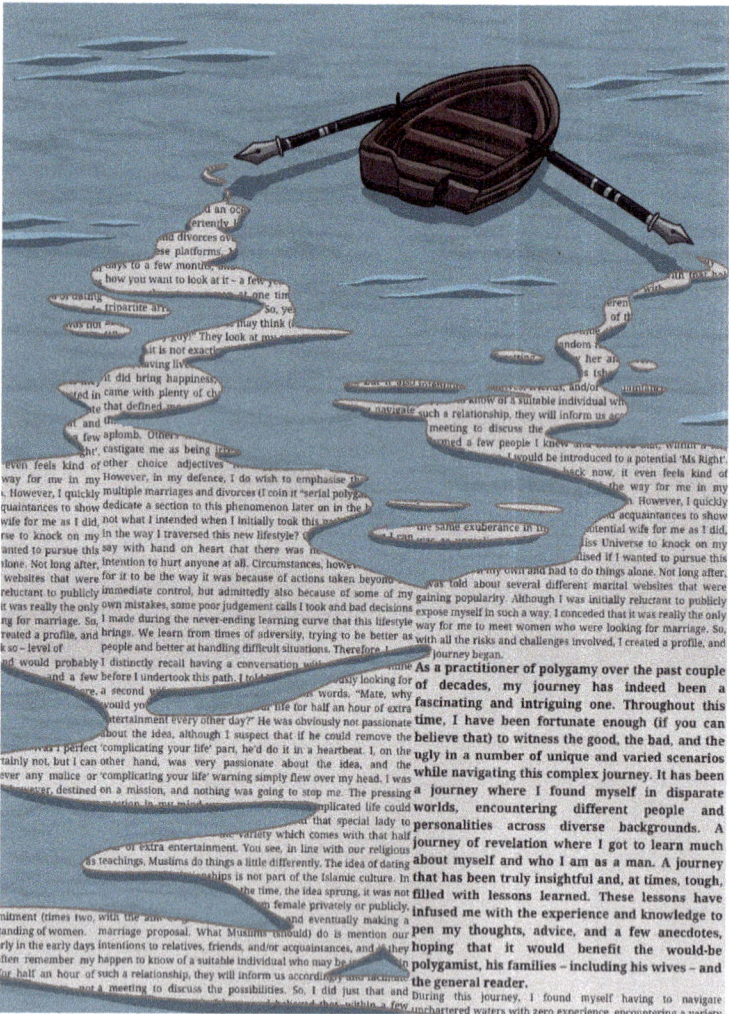

As a practitioner of polygamy over the past couple of decades, my journey has indeed been a fascinating and intriguing one. Throughout this time, I have been fortunate enough (if you can believe that) to witness the good, the bad, and the ugly in a number of unique and varied scenarios while navigating this complex journey. It has been a journey where I found myself in disparate worlds, encountering different people and personalities across diverse backgrounds. A journey of revelation where I got to learn much about myself and who I am as a man. A journey that has been truly insightful and, at times, tough, filled with lessons learned. These lessons have infused me with the experience and knowledge to pen my thoughts, advice, and a few anecdotes, hoping that it would benefit the would-be polygamist, his families – including his wives – and the general reader.

During this journey, I found myself having to navigate unchartered waters with zero experience, encountering a variety

CHAPTER 01

Personal Experiences & Anecdotes

As a practitioner of polygamy over the past couple of decades, my journey has indeed been a fascinating and intriguing one. Throughout this time, I have been fortunate enough (if you can believe that) to witness the good, the bad, and the ugly in a number of unique and varied scenarios while navigating this complex journey. It has been a journey where I found myself in disparate worlds, encountering different people and personalities across diverse backgrounds. A journey of revelation where I got to learn much about myself and who I am as a man. A journey that has been truly insightful and, at times, tough, filled with lessons learned. These lessons have infused me with the experience and knowledge to pen my thoughts, advice, and a few anecdotes, hoping that it would benefit the would-be polygamist, his families – including his wives – and the general reader.

I distinctly recall having a conversation with a friend of mine before I undertook this path. I told him I was seriously looking for a second wife, and I will never forget his words. "Mate, why would you want to complicate your life for half an hour of extra entertainment every other day?" He was obviously not passionate about the idea, although I suspect that if he could remove the 'complicating your life' part, he'd do it in a heartbeat.

I, on the other hand, was very passionate about the idea, and the 'complicating your life' warning simply flew over my head. I was on a mission, and nothing was going to stop me. The pressing question in my mind was not about how complicated life could be, but rather how and where do I find that special lady to enhance it and give me the variety which comes with that half hour of extra entertainment.

You see, in line with our religious teachings, Muslims do things a little differently. The idea of dating or pre-marital relationships is not part of the Islamic culture. In the society where I lived in at the time the idea sprung, it was not customary to approach any random female privately or publicly, with the aim of getting to know her and eventually making a marriage proposal. What Muslims (should) do is mention our intentions to relatives, friends, and/or acquaintances, and if they happen to know of a suitable individual who may be interested in such a relationship, they will inform us accordingly and facilitate a meeting to discuss the possibilities. So, I did just that and informed a few people I knew and believed that, within a few weeks, hey presto, I would be introduced to a potential 'Ms Right'. How naïve was I? Looking back now, it even feels kind of embarrassing. Nevertheless, it paved the way for me in my journey, and of course, we live, and we learn. However, I quickly concluded that expecting my friends and acquaintances to show the same exuberance in finding a potential wife for me as I did, was as unrealistic as expecting Miss Universe to knock on my door and offer to marry me. I realised if I wanted to pursue this path, I was on my own and had to do things alone. Not long after, I was told about several different marital websites that were gaining popularity. Although I was initially reluctant to publicly expose myself in such a way, I conceded that it was really the only way for me to meet women who were looking for marriage. So, with all the risks and challenges involved, I created a profile, and the journey began.

During this journey, I found myself having to navigate unchartered waters with zero experience, encountering a variety of personalities from different cultures, speaking different languages and across several geographies ranging from Asia to the Middle East, North Africa, Europe, and even extending to North and South America. The salient point to make is that there was success. It was truly exhilarating for me, and I felt like a fisherman who found an ocean full of fish.

The pitfall, however, was that it inadvertently led me to fall into a vicious cycle of marriages and divorces over the years with a number of women I met on these platforms. My marriages have lasted from a few days to a few months, and when I was fortunate – if fortune is how you want to look at it – a few years. I have also been married to more than two women at one time, dealing with a delicate tripartite arrangement situation.

So, yes, I have been around the block, and my male friends may think (some actually do), "Damn! What a lucky guy!" They look at my experience from the outside, although it is not exactly the way I would characterise it from the inside, having lived it. Don't get me wrong, there were times when it did bring happiness, joy and, yes, entertainment, but it also came with plenty of challenges and occasional grief. Challenges that defined me as a person and ultimately helped me navigate this journey with some – at least, I like to think so – level of aplomb.

Others may not see it this way and would probably castigate me as being irresponsible and insensitive, and a few other choice adjectives not appropriate to mention here. However, in my defence, I do wish to emphasise that being in multiple marriages and divorces (I coin it "serial polygamy" and dedicate a section to this phenomenon later on in the book) was not what I intended when I initially took this path. Was I perfect in the way I traversed this new lifestyle? Certainly not, but I can say with hand on heart that there was never any malice or intention to hurt anyone at all. Circumstances, however, destined for it to be the way it was because of actions taken beyond my immediate control, but admittedly also because of some of my own mistakes, some poor judgement calls I took and bad decisions I made during the never-ending learning curve that this lifestyle brings. We learn from times of adversity, trying to be better as people and better at handling difficult situations.

Therefore, I write this book with the sincere belief that my experiences have given me a unique and even nuanced insight into marriage, the responsibilities that accompany such a commitment (times two, three or four), and, dare I say, a better understanding of women.

Occasionally, it did take a toll on me, particularly in the early days when I was new to the journey. I would often remember my friend's quip about 'complicating your life for half an hour of extra entertainment' with a wry grin. Women are not uncomplicated creatures, and I had actually overlooked the fact that there were still another twenty-three and a half hours of the day to deal with. This brings me to an old joke that I am reminded of.

A Californian man was walking on a beach and saw a mysterious and elderly, sage-looking man in trouble. He helped him, and the grateful elderly man asked him to make a request so he could return the favour. He said, "I want a six-lane bridge to Hawaii so I can drive there every week."

The sage, frowning, replied, "That's impossible, young man, an architectural and engineering nightmare beyond my capabilities. Ask me something else!"

The man thought for a moment and said, "I wanna know the inner workings of a woman. Why do they cry? Why do they laugh? What makes them tick?"

The sagely looking man thought for a moment and, in a tone of resignation, said, "So how many lanes did you say you want in that bridge?"

But I digress! Back to my point.

The joke is old, but it may resonate with several men. My friend's words, unsurprisingly, did have their merits, with many unpredictable challenges I faced on the way.

So, the natural questions would be, "Why did you do it, bro?" and "Do you have any regrets?" My honest answer to the first question, "I was obsessed with the idea", and to the second, "Frankly, I do not believe in regrets!" Everything in life that happens to you is a lesson for you and, indeed, for others to learn from. Despite the 'making life complicated' axiom, there were also good times and cherished moments that helped me deal with much of the midlife crises men go through. Something I used to belittle as mythical, I later realised, was very real. The polygamy experiences have also shaped me in ways that gave me deep insights into how to navigate relationships with diverse personalities and different circumstances in the marriage landscape, where no two personalities or circumstances were identical; and this helped to render the task of dealing with married life and understanding women less complicated. It also left me with one profound thought that reverberates through my head: "Had I known then what I know now."

What I do know now is that marriage is a collaboration so unique actual hands-on experience in polygamy provides a solid benchmark to better understand, navigate, and manage relationships in a way that monogamy never can. I might get into trouble for saying this, but it's like trying to acclimatise your palate to different foods. No one can eat chicken and rice every day, right? I've been there and done that, so trust me and trust the process that this book is all about.

There is a caveat, though. It has to be done right, and often, the idea of doing it right can be convoluted. When not done right, no amount of artistry can turn it into a pretty picture. Indeed, things can degenerate quickly and get quite ugly. The guilty party will inevitably be seen as the man, and quite frankly, in many instances, this would be true. Not because he ventured into this practice and lifestyle per se but because he may have bitten off considerably more than he could chew. I will endeavour to outline all possible scenarios in my book to guide those who wish to tread this path and understand what the 'doing it right' mantra means, and then provide suggestions and techniques on how to bring it to life. Advanced insights into these techniques can help avoid mistakes and pitfalls that men can easily fall into but could have easily avoided as well.

Warning! No matter how successful you think you may have been in adopting these techniques, there is no guarantee that you will not be spared of blame. It is what it is, and you chose the path that you chose.

It is not my intention to make this book a biography of my life (yawn). However, I do wish to touch on and indirectly allude to some aspects of my experiences in order for you to understand some of the situations you will be confronted with and the decisions you will need to make if you wish to seriously consider polygamy as a lifestyle.

Remember - and allow me to be a little philosophical here for a bit - there is always a context behind what we decide to do or not do in our lives. Things that happen are sometimes connected to past experiences and, many times, because of circumstances we are faced with at any given moment. I was happy with my married life, but I was also yearning for more within the boundaries of my religious beliefs and teachings. When I discovered the rare instances of other men in polygamous relationships, I saw an alternative lifestyle that I was impressed with and fascinated by. I wanted that lifestyle. It looked so macho, and I, naively at the time, wanted to be macho. Undoubtedly, I had a few obstacles in my way - family, my new wife, insufficient money, and lack of testicular fortitude. And trust me, you need the last two in ample supply. So, for many years, I had to put the idea at the very back of my head and dream about what it would be like for me. Eventually of course, I did find out.

I wouldn't be forthright if I didn't admit that there were moments when I questioned my decision to continue with this lifestyle. Then I snapped out of it, moved on, and my journey began. That is all I am prepared to say about my personal experiences.

So, what have I learned about marriage, relationships, and women through my experiences in polygamy and how to navigate this lifestyle during the times of calm and storm? The following chapters provide my perspectives, insights, thoughts, and guidelines based on anecdotes and real-life experiences, including from other men who have lived similar lifestyles. I hope you find these stories thought-provoking, entertaining, and enjoyable. Of course, I do recognise that there might be critics and antagonists who will vehemently disagree and be infuriated by some of the content in this book and the "controversial" contentions I make. Not everyone is going to be happy with me or my views, but not everyone needs to be. You do you and let them do them.

Regardless, I am confident I can help you understand what polygamy entails and provide you with insights that may not be immediately obvious as you contemplate your next steps, if there are any (wink). For those of you who have no plans for that "next step", I still encourage you to read the book and imagine what it would feel like. Because we all know you would if you could!

CHAPTER 02

Men, Women, &
Physical Desires

Pardon me for stating the obvious, but men and women are not equal. They are wired differently when it comes to physical desires, and insofar as they relate to aspects of marriage and relationships, they really do not operate at the same wavelength. Women tend to be more emotional and need to feel desired, loved, and taken care of. Men are visual creatures by nature and have stronger physical needs. Bluntly speaking, they crave sexual intimacy. Understanding this is the key to understanding why polygamy is a meaningful alternative to infidelity. Let's talk about this a little.

Gender Equality Or Gender Equity?

Those who call themselves progressive will try to convince you that the idea of men and women not being equal is an antiquated notion that, according to them, only serves to degrade the value of women and treat them as inferior to men. To them, men and women are fundamentally equal in so many areas of life and, therefore, should be treated equally, and anyone saying otherwise is nothing but a misogynist or a borderline one. "Gender Equality" is the phrase you hear time and time again with this "in your face" propagandising that attempts to question your sensibilities or even integrity if you somehow oppose the idea, wholly or even partially. I, myself, do not buy into this fallacy or the propaganda. A cursory look at any kind of peer-reviewed scientific study clearly demarcates and identifies significant and fundamental differences. And in all honesty, you don't even need studies to understand this truth. Anyone who has grown up in a family with male and female siblings, as I did, will know most things there are to know about multiple personalities and mood swings. Don't believe me? Ask my brothers-in-law. Jokes aside, it's really not rocket science.

Obviously, no one claims that there are absolutely no similarities and equal treatment is never warranted. Both genders must eat, sleep, and pay taxes. So, equality is justified at times, but – and here's the caveat - only when equity and justice prevail. And this, my dear readers, is a critical benchmark to recognise. Gender equality is basically impractical in its essence because equality may not always mean equity. The paradigm must shift to something sensible and practical, and here I (and a Google search) introduce you to the concept of "Gender Equity" to replace this impractical and, quite frankly, nonsensical notion of absolute equality.

Gender Equity, according to Sol Fauquier from Common Goal (a global impact movement for the world of football), "goes beyond gender equality to address the specific needs and challenges of different genders. Two important words used in this description are "needs" and "challenges", and indeed, paying attention and focusing on them is important in guiding our understanding of how men and women are wired differently and why polygamy is an important practice in fulfilling these gender-based needs and challenges. To explore this further, let's first touch on the subject of promiscuity - among both men and women.

Promiscuity Among Men

Sexual behavioural patterns between the genders, suggests to us with very little doubt that societies from time immemorial have seen that – you guessed it – men have a promiscuity level significantly higher than women. An axiomatic truth? For all intents and purposes, yes! Some may produce obscure modern-day statistics attempting to challenge this reality, but it really is not a tenable position to take seriously if we were to ponder meaningfully at what we have witnessed, even in recent times. After all, the "MeToo" movement was not about men being sexually harassed, was it? So, I believe anyone with even a basic understanding of the man's psyche must acknowledge this essentially irrefutable truth.

Now that we have established and acknowledged that the testosterone levels in men are higher, we can better understand what motivates men when it comes to relationships with the opposite gender. Steve Harvey, the famous American television personality, said in his book, "Straight, No Chaser" that he sets out to "Get rid of [the] myth that men and women can be friends." Talking to another TV Hostess, he said, *"You're an attractive woman. There's some guy somewhere saying, 'Yeah, we're friends.' No! He's your friend only because you have made it absolutely clear that nothing else is happening except for this friendship we have. We remain your friends in hopes that one day there'll be a crack in the door, a chink in the armour... trust and believe that guy that you think is just your buddy — he will slide in that crack the moment he gets the opportunity because we're guys."* The primary motivation for men in a relationship with a woman is physical intimacy. This is what they want, this is what they seek (at times even predatorily), and this is what they need, even if they cannot always have it.

Is that the only thing they need? To some men, yes, that's all. However, it is obviously not across the board, and any cursory understanding of human psychology teaches us that human interaction does extend beyond the physical. Companionship, emotional security, sharing life events, procreation, and other social norms and behaviour patterns in human society play an important role in shaping our lives to achieve happiness. Yet, for men, the primary objective (not necessarily the most important) is what it is! And indeed, they do attempt to slide into any crack that Harvey speaks about as often as possible, consensually, for the most part, but sometimes, unfortunately, coercively.

Challenges For Muslim Men

For the Muslim man, the challenge he faces in fulfilling this need is a little different. Casual flings and illicit affairs are strictly prohibited in

Islam, whether he is married or not. Here, my non-Muslim friends will be quicker than a gun-slinging cowboy to remind me about how they know of many married Mohameds and Ahmeds and Abdullahs who brazenly flout the prohibition and don't blink an eyelid while doing so. It is usually their "gotcha" moment, and admittedly, they would not be wrong. Indeed, many Muslim men, married and unmarried, do engage in illicit arrangements. Without being judgemental or sanctimonious because no one is perfect, they do this because it requires time, energy and, of course, lots of money to support wives and offspring in a legitimate relationship, and they do not want to "inconvenience" themselves with such burdens, preferring the illicit route to that 'half-hour of extra entertainment'. In fact, on one occasion, an acquaintance of mine suggested, and I am paraphrasing here, "Why trouble yourself with that burden (of marrying another woman) when you can get the entertainment you want with minimal time and energy and a heck of a lot less money if you go to such and such district?" I politely declined.

And like me, there are a significant number of Muslim men who do take the prohibition seriously and do not engage in flings or illicit affairs. They are loyal to the tenets of their beliefs and loyal to their families. Kudos to them. Yet, virtually all of them, with few exceptions, fantasise at the thought of experiencing intimacy with different partners because that is what men seek and, I repeat, in many cases, need.

Another challenge that he will need to tackle is his first wife's reaction once she becomes aware of what he intends to do; or finds out when he does it. If he is not prepared and ready for the proverbial to hit the fan – and when it does hit, it can get pretty ugly – it would be catastrophic. How he navigates this situation is explored later.

Promiscuity Among Women

Women are different from men when it comes to promiscuity. Any sensible and unbiased thinker should acknowledge this, although current trends may suggest that the promiscuity "gap" between the genders appears to be narrowing. Yet, any studies that are conducted continue to confirm that men do substantially exceed in levels of promiscuity, thus proving their innate obsessive nature time and time again. No prizes, guys, for this achievement.

So why are we seeing this surge? My take is the following. Times have changed, and times are changing. From the middle of the 20th century, with the acceleration of technological advancements, the world has become a much smaller place, figuratively speaking. We used to learn about societies and cultures different from our own from books and stories told by intrepid adventurers who 'went to explore strange new worlds, to seek out new life and civilisations, and to boldly go where no man has gone before' (for you fans of Star Trek). Nowadays, information about other cultures and behaviours is instantly accessible in the palms of our hands via our smartphones. The so-called progressive societies, dominant in relation to promoting their values, have essentially divorced themselves from traditionalism and adopted secular democratic liberal values, which in many instances are the antithesis of the once cherished traditions (including in aspects of sexuality and sexual behavioural patterns). Exposure to such liberal values and behaviour plays an important role in the hearts, minds and actions of men and women, and it comes as no surprise if more and more people are tempted towards practices that were once considered taboo but have now been normalised in society. Women are equally lured by such temptations.

However, in the essence of her being, a woman is dedicated and loyal to one man, can only truly love one man, and has no need or joy in being with any other man at the same time. Deep down, they know this to be true, even if current trends show a slight shift. As I alluded to earlier, rules and regulations are not formulated with the exceptions in mind.

Challenges For Women

For a woman facing the prospect of her husband marrying another woman, or two or three, she will undergo a myriad of emotions that tear into the very fabric of her being. A vicissitude in her circumstances leaves her with a sense of helplessness and hopelessness and a temptation to crawl under a rock to remove herself from what feels like a nightmare. Notwithstanding feelings of intense jealousy and betrayal, her life will turn upside down with emotions of anger and sadness simultaneously permeating her whole demeanour. She will start questioning her value as a woman, and this may manifest in sudden mood swings and poor treatment of those around her, including perhaps her children.

Dealing with her emotions will be hard enough, but she will also have to now deal with the "other" woman in her life. And through no fault of her own, this other woman will likely become public enemy number one in the eyes of everyone sympathetic to the first wife. I will explore in more detail the plight of both the first and second wives in other chapters. However, the intent, for now, is to convey the magnitude and intensity of the emotional plight of women who are put in this situation, not because she asked for it, but because many men are simply unable to think north of their naval. Men are, after all, men.

Are men who enter such a relationship to blame? You would think the picture I painted would naturally suggest that it is indeed his fault, and therefore the answer to this question would be a resounding "YES!" However, what this book hopes to achieve is a modicum of understanding, showing that a man is not going outside of his innate nature in desiring and subsequently marrying more than one woman. Hence, he is really not to be blamed. Having said that, it does not remove him from the responsibility to deal with the consequences of his actions because of the decisions he made.

Takeaway

Men and women have not been created equal, and therefore, the natural laws set in place for their functioning in society will not be equal. Men have traditionally been the financial providers for their wives and families. Women do not have that obligation. It's not equal, but it works fine because it does so within their God-given nature. For the same reason, polygamy has primarily been a male domain throughout much of history, and it has worked fine because it does so within that God-given nature. Don't fight it.

CHAPTER 03

Practice Of Polygamy

Polygamy is not a new phenomenon, nor is it one that was introduced by Muslims. It has been practised since pre-biblical times and was part of societal norms without any kind of taboo attached to it. At the advent of Islam, it was not the case that men were marrying one woman, and then Islam introduced the law that permitted them to have up to four wives. This is a myth. In fact, religious and historical literature suggests that men were married to a dozen if not more, women at the same time. Indeed, other societies, ancient and not so ancient, also observed this practice as a norm without any contention or fiery objections. Islam merely restricted it to four at any one time with a stringent set of responsibilities obligated upon men who opted to do so. And this is an important point to mention. It is an option, not an obligation. Contrary to popular notion, it is hard work to take responsibility for additional families that inevitably includes plenty of rugrats (a.k.a. children) running around. Bank balances of such men are never five figures.

The issue we face in our times is that certain ideologies are looked upon unfavourably through a modern-day lens, and derogatory judgements are made without understanding the context of these ideologies in terms of the era they emanate from and the societies that lived in those times. In my opinion, this is a travesty of justice brought about by a mind-set that promotes supremacist ideologies denigrating values not shared by them as inferior. Short rant over.

Why Is Polygamy A Societal Taboo?

A practice that is taboo is one that is prohibited or restricted by social custom. As I mentioned, the practice of polygamy was never considered taboo for the longest of time. This changed possibly sometime around the twentieth century and likely around the time when traditionalism was replaced by secular liberal values, which became dominant in much of the first world. Societies that upheld these values were eager to export them to the rest of the world. And guess what? Much of the rest of the world accepted them to varying degrees.

The values promoted by secularism are a vast topic and certainly not appropriate for the purpose of this book except to draw the reader's attention to its influence on the way marriage and relationships have evolved. Polygamy has transformed, astonishingly, from a normal, acceptable institution in societies of the not-too-distant past to a modern-day taboo of such magnitude that it has literally been made illegal in many Western societies. Why is this astonishing? Well, the reality is that, in these societies, entering into a relationship with more than one woman and giving them a life by providing them with all the essentials they require – accommodation, financial and emotional support and security for the rest of their lives – is considered illegal if the woman is designated as a "wife". Not if she is a "girlfriend" or "mistress"! Let that sink in for a minute. You could potentially be jailed for being in a second marital relationship, but not if that relationship is an adulterous illicit affair. Make sense of that one for me if you can.

This transformation has infiltrated even the minds of Muslims, whose societies have also "progressed" in accepting the idea that men should only be married to one woman, and more than one is an unfathomable "crime" deserving of community and family ostracisation. In fact, a few male friends have told me personally how their wives prefer that they entertain themselves with casual one-night flings, even if they have to pay for it, rather than marry legitimately and take on a noble and even sacred responsibility. That says something very revealing about the intense feelings flaming this objection. It also demonstrates a virulent dichotomy between the man's obsession with women and the desire to experience variety; and a woman's objection and remonstration to share their husband in marriage, which is worth exploring in a little more detail. But before that, let me share with you another humorous anecdote:

An Egyptian man living in ancient times in an authoritarian kingdom came home sobbing profusely with tears streaming down his face. His wife, worried and concerned, asked him what the matter was. With his head down and voice breaking, he replied, "The king ordered all the men in his kingdom to marry a second wife or face execution" Without blinking, the wife said, "That's wonderful news!" Her husband propped his head up and, with a puzzled and almost hopeful look in his eyes, asked, "You don't mind?" "Of course, not", she responded, "You will be a shaheed!" (Martyr)

The story is obviously fictional, but the sentiment depicting that fiery objection to polygamy is not.

The Dichotomy Between Obsession And Objection

A relationship between a husband and a wife is truly unique. In a happy marriage, what they share as soulmates is something special and can never be replicated in any other relationship humans experience in their lives. They are essentially ONE! The desire for the husband to then marry another woman tests the very foundations of that relationship to the core, and the question legitimately asked is, "Why test it?" Why can man not be content and happy with his soulmate?

The reason is quite simple, even if it is contentious. It goes back to what Steve Harvey said about sliding into the crack if any opportunity arises, and quite frankly, at times, that crack is forcefully (and illegitimately) open. This stems from and **has much to do with the innate obsession men have for women.** An obsession aggravated by the objectification of women in modern society through various communication channels readily available to men. An obsession that many women simply do not understand, nor can they empathise with, and therefore react with such hostile opposition. And finally, an obsession so deep that a significant number of men are indeed ready to 'complicate their lives for that half an hour of extra entertainment' because of it.

At the opposite end of the spectrum, you have intense levels of love and possessiveness a woman feels for her husband, which may surpass anything that she had experienced before. Ponder this: A woman devotes her entire married life to making her husband happy and surrenders every fibre of her being for his gratification. Her innocence is a very special commodity and so precious that it would **not** be something that she would offer to just any man. She gives away herself with the sincerest of intentions and the purity of love for her man. It then becomes natural for her to feel a monumental sense of betrayal and disbelief when she finds herself in a situation that she did not ask for.

Personally, my experiences suggest that these passions permeating in each spouse have an intensity level that can only be understood at a very deep-rooted biological level. In other words, women, because they are women, simply cannot fathom the obsession that men have for other women. And men, because they are men, simply cannot feel or understand the depth and intensity of love their wives feel for them, showcased by her fierce resistance to sharing him with another.

The impasse is real and divide-wide, which is why any actions that are carried out need to be thought out carefully and with consideration. Otherwise, the consequences can be devastating. Let us explore in an authentic and forthright way how to come closer to understanding why men need to marry more than one wife and why, in some instances, they should be allowed to do so.

What's Love Got To Do With It?

Honestly speaking, absolutely nothing. Forgive me for my candour, but love has virtually nothing to do with men embarking on the polygamy journey. Someone once wrote in a popular song that love is a second-hand emotion. When I read this description and understood what was intended, I thought to myself that it had serious merit, particularly in the context of polygamy. A man does not want a second wife because he wants to find someone else to love, other than his first wife. This is not the motive or what he was thinking when initially exploring the idea. He could be completely and madly in love with his first wife yet still lust for other women.

If Not Love Then It Must Be Lust

Is it about lust? Before answering this, let's get one thing out of the way. Lust is not a dirty nor should it be considered a shameful word. It is a natural biological phenomenon that is instilled in every human being, usually starting at puberty. It is quite comical when antagonists accuse you of being an impure, lustful person because you want to marry another woman as if this is not part of their nature also. I have personally encountered a few such antagonists who, while married to their only wives and vehemently chastising the polygamist for his lifestyle choice, unashamedly engage in secretive and sordid affairs with different women. Comical and hypocritical are two words that come to mind!

What is truly impure is if you channel this lust in ways that are dishonourable and ignoble, hurting others in the process. I have argued polygamy is not that. So, let's ask the question again, "Is it about lust?" Yes, it almost always is, and as shocking and radical as that sounds, it is just the plain and inescapable truth. Facts are insensitive to our feelings. Admittedly, other reasons exist, and they are certainly not unimportant. For example, if a man desires more children and does not want to burden his first wife with that difficult responsibility, polygamy provides an avenue to achieve this. It's also possible that he believes there may be an intellectual gap – either superior or inferior – between him and his first wife, negatively affecting the vigour in their relationship. He then pursues polygamy to fill that gap.

However, it is man's innate nature driven by lust that is the paramount feature in his polygamous desire. Allowing him the leeway to fulfil it responsibly and honourably must be seriously considered as a legitimate alternative to illicit arrangements, which society unanimously agrees is irresponsible and reprehensible. If he is prevented from taking the responsible path, the temptation to take an illicit one may occupy his mind, and if he does fall astray, then nothing good will come from such egregious misdemeanours. This is not uncommon, and we hear of many marriages breaking down because of the husband's callous infidelity.

Notwithstanding the existence of lust, it does not preclude the possibility that love could and should play an important part in the second marriage of a man. When a man is involved with another woman in a responsible and legitimate way, love will naturally develop, grow, and flourish; and it is a critical component in sustaining the new relationship and making it successful. Women feed off emotions and demonstrating that you do have a deep affection for her, with words and deeds, cements that psychological security she must have to be able to give back to the relationship. And oftentimes, she will give back a lot more than she takes.

Takeaway

Something that may not be popular in a society does not necessarily qualify it to be detrimental and bad. Sometimes, we need to endure a little pain for the greater good. Going to the dentist is not fun, but it's got to be done at times. Similarly, the practice of polygamy can cause hurt, yet it can also help to prevent greater hurt when illicit alternatives become the acceptable norm in society. The need for men to take conscious responsibility for the choices they make will also play an important role in the success of their polygamous lifestyle. While lust may have got you to where you are, love and dedication to commitment will help you to stay in that place peacefully. So, when marrying again, choose wisely and find someone with the connection and chemistry that is required to take it to the next level. And if she is rich, that's a bonus!

CHAPTER 04

Setting The Stage

When you make the conscious decision to pursue the path leading towards polygamy, many factors will come into play. Some factors you may be able to predict while many unknowns will crop up that you must fumble through. Speculating what is around the corner is almost always impossible. Also, be prepared to face the consequences of utter miscalculations stemming from your own expectations. This happens, and it is purely your fault, and you will have to dig yourself out of that hole when and if things go south. So, some of the factors that you will need to understand and questions you may need to address and navigate around are outlined in the following pages.

Mid-Life Crisis

Something I was told I suffered from (and subtly accused of) when I considered polygamy was that of having a mid-life crisis, not least by those closest to me. Apparently, a mid-life crisis starts at around the age of forty, so the subtle inference here is that men wake up on their fortieth birthday and realise something has been missing all their lives, and BINGO, a sudden interest in women surfaces then and only then! I don't think anyone seriously believes this, but if you do, then I have real estate on Mars to sell! A vibrant man, if he is brutally honest, will tell you this is a load of bunkum. The obsession with women starts at a very young age, and it does not end, ever. Believe it or not, accept it or not and deny it all you want; it's simply reality.

No doubt mid-life crises are real, and we should never underplay their significance nor how they affect almost everyone to varying degrees. Mental health and well-being are not to be taken lightly, and it is imperative that we all find ways to overcome the negative psychological impact that manifests during our advancing years. The notion that our time in this world is finite does dawn on us as we age, and let's be forthright about it – the thought is certainly a frightening one. Find some solace in getting closer to your Creator and realising that meeting with Him is inevitable. There is nothing more tranquil. At the same time, I do wholeheartedly advocate finding passions to help you maintain an upbeat and feel-good demeanour as you grow older. Spend more time with family, pick up a hobby, play a sport, travel the world and yes, if favourable circumstances present themselves, marry another woman. And I don't say this with nonchalance. For the men who have the ability to do so, if indeed mid-life crisis is bringing you down and causing lethargy, experience the exuberance of being in a relationship with another woman, and then watch how your demeanour elevates to levels you thought have long been lost and buried in your youth. I would also venture to say that your relationship with your first wife could potentially see a surge in positive intensity, and some factors behind this will be discussed later. Miracles can and do happen.

Favourable Scenarios & Obstacles

To set the stage for you to embark on the polygamy journey, let me introduce you to the kind of environment and circumstances that should ideally be in place to help you on the way. Some obvious and others less so. A conducive environment puts you in the right frame of mind and allows you to embark on this journey with some semblance of peace and tranquillity. If these circumstances are absent, they become, by default, obstacles in your path, and you can virtually write off peace and tranquillity as unobtainable. Obstacles are not always easy to remove. However, with a teaspoon of determination, a cup of patience and bucket loads of wisdom, it can be done.

• Financial Stability Is Essential

In the introduction, I mentioned that the title for this book was taken from a verse found in the Qur'an, "Marry two, three or four but..." and naturally leaves you asking the question, "But what?" While there are indeed many 'buts' to consider, some obvious and some subtle, the one specific to the verse is a conditional 'but', referring to the man's ability to be equitable between his wives, specifically in relation to financial support, time management and kind treatment. In Islam, it is the sole duty of the husband to provide financially for his wives and family, even if his wives happen to be millionaires. She may volunteer out of the goodness of her heart to contribute to the financial upkeep of the family, but she is not obliged to do so and should never be coerced to in any way. Therefore, this burden falls squarely on the shoulders of men, so – sorry guys - if you can't afford more than one wife, you can't marry more than one wife, or as they say in Hong Kong, "No money, no talk!"

There is a reason why I put financial stability at the top of the list of favourable circumstances. It is a critically important point to understand and embrace. Marriage is a serious commitment and definitely not a free ride. Financial support for the average guy is difficult itself when it comes to one wife and family, let alone more than one. And what exactly is financial support? It's the ability to maintain separate households for each wife/family and all of the 'trimmings' that come with it. Rent, school/university fees, groceries, clothing, holidays, medical costs, and the list goes on. In addition, if you plan to buy a gift for one wife, you are obliged to be equal with the other missus too and buy her the same gift or another one of a similar value. It's not so easy, is it? Go on, confess! You didn't think about all of this, did you? Why? Because it was always about that 'half hour of extra entertainment.'

In the context of marriage, Muslim men are taught that if they want to marry but are unable to support a wife, they may delay the marriage until such time they have the means. Meanwhile, fasting is encouraged as an effective way to curb our physical desires and avoid falling into sinful actions. What this means is simple - if your finances are not up to speed, drop the idea completely and take up voluntary fasting. I am not joking. All too often, men, being men, hastily enter into what they believe will be some kind of glossy lifestyle where they will actually and finally experience what they have long dreamt of. The dream may come true, but the gloss dampens when the reality of married life sets in, and bills start to pile up. It's at that point you come to realise the financial implications of what you have entered into and begin to think that maybe, just maybe, you have bitten off way more than you can chew. In a marriage, finances can be a real sticking point, particularly if your wife senses that her rights have been infringed upon and neglected. That can happen in a monogamous marriage, so what do you think could happen if you add two, three or four?

Therefore, before the idea of polygamy even enters your mind, ensure you have sufficient finances and more to be able to maintain a reasonable standard of living and steer away from financial problems that can easily break down the relationship and cause unwarranted spousal friction. If it requires time for you to increase your net asset value in order to be able to handle the responsibility, then take that time. Remember, happy wife, happy life!

As for the question of how much is sufficient, it depends entirely on your lifestyle and circumstances. The rule of thumb: prioritise what you **can do** over what you **want to do.**

• Maintaining Separate Households

Included in financial stability is the ability to maintain separate households for your wives. Islamic law affords each wife the right to have her own home. Either by renting or buying, depending on the husband's financial health. In some ultra-conservative Muslim societies, however, custom dictates that wives of one man share the same home. Strange as that may be from our lenses, it actually works for them, mainly because polygamy is not so uncommon in those societies, having been practised for several generations. If you are not coming from such societies, don't even think about it. This is not going to work for you.

Your first wife has the right and will demand that, if you want to bring another woman into your life, make sure that this woman is given her own accommodation because unicorns will take over the world before she agrees to share her home with your number two. And when she tells you this, don't you dare get upset, offended or angry. And if you do feel anger, show her with an Oscar-winning performance that you are not.

Why is this an important point to emphasise? Simply put, what she won't see won't hurt her, and one of your important objectives in establishing that conducive environment is to not cause more hurt than you already have. Having both wives share the same home will not only compound that hurt but open the door for potential conflict between your spouses. You have heard the proverb "Hell hath no fury like a woman scorned", right? Now multiply that by two and imagine what it would be like. So, if you have such a ludicrous idea, give it up.

No Objection From Family Members

For any man who wishes to enter a polygamous relationship, the support of your family, or at least a bona fide "no objection" from them, does help to create an atmosphere that allows you to pursue your desire pretty much free of stress. The family I am talking about here is everyone directly connected to you and affected by your actions, except your first wife. She deserves a section of her own, being the cornerstone of your life. Other immediate family members are without doubt important, too. Virtually everything we do centres around these people and contributes to their physical and mental well-being. And vice versa.

Family structures across various cultures and geographies have different sensibilities and need to be dealt with according to their own set of cultural dynamics. However, generally, in the journey of life, priorities, responsibilities, and focus shift over time, and each individual is responsible for finding his or her own path to happiness and contentment. For Muslims, of course, this must be done within the framework of their religious teachings.

However, a single and important message must be instilled in the minds of affected family members. And that is, this is **your life** – not theirs – to live, and **your desire** – not theirs – to act upon in a responsible and noble way, ultimately for **your own** happiness. The alternative (to polygamy) is irresponsible and ignoble. This may sound like a polite way of saying 'mind your own business', and in a sense, it is, but it is necessary to draw some boundaries quickly and early on in your journey.

While family members are important, the impact of your actions affects each group differently. The list below aims to identify each sub-group of families ranked in order of most highly affected to the least. I have selected five groups that, in my experience, are exposed one way or another.

1. Children
2. In-Laws
3. Parents
4. Siblings
5. Other relatives

While you talk this talk of maintaining interaction, commitment, and affection, once you plunge into the new lifestyle, it is imperative that you walk the walk, and this applies most importantly to the first group on the list: your children. I have devoted another chapter titled "What

About The Kids?" in order to share experiences in dealing with them and their emotions.

For your in-laws, their primary concern will naturally be their daughter and the fact that you (from their perspective) have uprooted the very foundations of her life and possibly caused irreparable psychological damage. Sometimes, to them, even more so than to her. It may possibly be easier on them if her father is or had been married to two or more women at some point in time. In some instances, however, fathers accept it for themselves but strongly object to the idea when it comes to their daughters. Fatherly love and protection, or hypocritical behaviour? You decide!

As for your parents, their concern will be your reputation (and, by extension, theirs) in the community when the "scandal" of your other marriage is brought to light. They may have to hear how insensitive and cruel you are, what a badly brought up child you are, and all sorts of other gossip-fuelled rumours fitting for fairy stories. You should not let such talk distract you from your course of action and give confidence to your parents that you have not, are not and will not transgress any limits, particularly limits set by God. What people then say negatively won't really matter.

Dealing with the elders is a delicate matter that requires wisdom and patience, more so in the early days of this sudden life-changing event. So, walking that walk is important here, and giving them time to adjust to the new normal goes without saying. Patience, kindness, showing empathy and then more patience are the way forward and must be your new mantra, and better days will come......trust me!

Siblings and other relatives are probably the easiest to deal with because, in reality, *it is not* their business. They do not have a horse in this race, and if anything, they may exhibit surprise and curiosity, and perhaps the males among them will be a little envious, but tensions with them will be almost non-existent.

The Sentiments Of Your First Wife

I have described the involvement of your first wife in your polygamy journey and how to navigate her emotions and reactions in a separate chapter. For now, it's about setting the stage and positioning yourself in front of her sans animosity.

This will be a significant obstacle to overcome. You have two options – the sneaky approach by going ahead with your plans without her knowledge or a forthright one to work on her objection through patient dialogue and discussion. I discuss the circumstances where the former may become necessary for you in the chapter entitled "Your First Wife". However, I make an important disclaimer here. Not informing your wife must be an absolute last resort, having earnestly tried every other possibility to convince her.

Bear in mind that your first wife is the single most important person affected by your decision to marry again. Her sentiments are paramount, and her opinion needs to matter. At this juncture, you should understand that it is not necessary for her to support you overtly in your endeavours. She will neither like nor embrace your plans to be with another woman, and it would be audacious of you to expect that from her. However, part of that conducive environment you will require for your escapade is a non-virulent, non-objectionable wife in your corner, even if it is from a distance. This will go a considerable way to placating any animosity felt by other family members, in particular your children and in-laws.

Helping your wife reach such levels of stoicism is never going to be easy, and much will depend on her own individual personality, her upbringing and, if she is religious, her level of faith. It requires you to maintain an open channel of communication that allows her to express her raw emotions without inhibition. She may want to rant, and as long as it is within the privacy of your own confines, she should absolutely be given that space to do so. If you have a sarcastic tendency, like I do, this would not be the best time to exhibit it. Never forget that while you are gaining something in your life, she is losing part of it. So, in those moments, you have to be sensitive to her emotional plight and will just have to shut your mouth and accept the barrage of possible abuse headed your way. Verbal and perhaps (lightly) physical.

In time, when the dust settles and *it will settle*, you will then need to assure her of certain things. Don't be a nincompoop saying things like 'Nothing will change, darling' unless you take pleasure in having your face visited by her palms at a speed of knots. Such a statement is patronising and insulting to her intelligence and, frankly, not true. Of course, things *will* change, and they will change drastically for all of you in different ways. Failure to realise and acknowledge that is psychological suicide. Therefore, your primary objective at this juncture is to assure her that what will never change is your commitment to her and your family. Convince her of that first and foremost. Your testosterone hormone will silently thank you for it.

Monetary incentives and gifts will help. No, it is not a bribe per se, but an understanding that material incentives have a place in the happiness of all of us. Contrary to that popular benevolent adage, money *does* bring the average person happiness to a certain, and I would argue, a large degree. So, as much as you can, shower her lavishly with gifts, take her on a holiday, or take her for an umrah (lesser pilgrimage to Mecca).

After all this, it is critical you demonstrate that you meant what you said and not merely empty words or promises. In time, the situation will ease and improve. It will never be the same, but it will be a new normal, and believe it or not, it can even be rewarding for all concerned.

Therefore, the dignified and respectable way to tackle this obstacle and transform it to your advantage is the dialogue approach and taking pains to make sense of why you want another wife. Climbing Mount Everest? Maybe, but you may surprise yourself as you learn how reasonable conversation, combined with repeated re-assurances, can sometimes produce that light at the end of the tunnel, albeit infinitesimal at first sight. Don't give up.

Courage & Fortitude

It's quite simple, really, and there is no polite way to say this without being impactful. You need balls! If you don't have them, don't even think about doing this. The steady stream of criticism and antagonism will intensify over time and potentially culminate in a crescendo of accusations, allegations, and insults. You need to be thick-skinned enough to avoid crumbling into a state of doubt and uncertainty viz-a-viz your intended path forward. At the same time, you should not allow that thick skin to make you insensitive to the feelings of those who are directly affected by your actions. Here, I will briefly explore a couple of scenarios that you may encounter that will require this courage and fortitude.

• When Informing Your Wife

The lead up to the moment you decide to tell your wife and other family members, will likely be nerve-racking. You may have been thinking about polygamy for some time, perhaps even years. You will have reached a point when you have firmly made the decision to find a second wife, and there is absolutely no talking you out of it. This is when you must muster the courage to inform those whom you consider important enough to know if, indeed, you do plan to tell people – there are men who do not inform their family at the outset, which requires another discussion. When you do sit down to tell them, be honest and truthful and deal with their reaction calmly and wisely.

• *The Day of Your Wedding*

The day has finally come, and you are about to embark on this journey. You will be faced with a myriad of emotions, from excitement and nervousness to apprehension and fear of the unknown. In the mix of these emotions, you will likely feel a sense of intense guilt for what your first wife and family are going through as you say, "I do" for the second time. Doubts may creep in, and second thoughts will reverberate through your entire being. However, this is what you desired and what you strove for, having finally arrived at the place you want to be. Keep reminding yourself that you did not commit any transgression against yourself or your family. You were upfront and honest with what you wanted, and you maintained your dignity throughout, with your forthright behaviour and sincere commitment to all affected parties. Moreover, you have also committed yourself to an additional human being, your new bride, who also possesses feelings and emotions. Not everyone is going to sympathise with or even recognise the emotions that you are experiencing, yet it's at this time you have to be steadfast and not falter. It is at this time you need to take that leap of faith and make it work.

When Everything Else Fails

When all your efforts and strategies fail, and you find yourself in an impossible situation, it is then time to throw in the towel. The 'extra half-hour of entertainment' dream you so desperately desired is over, and you need to move onto something that will not necessarily replace the dream but occupy your mind sufficiently enough to overcome that obsession you have nurtured for so long. Ponder this: You don't have sufficient money, your family members are overtly and vehemently objecting, and your first wife has virtually abandoned you. So, where in the world do you expect to find the courage and fortitude to embark on this endeavour with your back against this monumental metaphoric wall? The physical and emotional toll is not worth it. You then have two choices: give up the idea entirely as suggested or fall into illicit relationships that will end up destroying your life. The latter can never be an option.

Takeaway

In life, there are many things we want to do but are unable to do for a variety of reasons. In the case of polygamy, something that's already considered a radical action by many in society, if you do not or are unable to set the stage for an environment that allows you to traverse the journey relatively stress-free, your ultimate goal of achieving contentment and happiness will be compromised. Work towards creating favourable circumstances if you are serious and be patient, mature and wise during the process as you deal with those closest to you and who will be affected most. But if these circumstances are not, in fact, favourable but rather obstacles you will find extremely difficult to overcome, then give up the idea and take up, yes, you guessed right, voluntary fasting. The family and stability that you currently have and cherish are infinitely better than if you don't have any of that.

CHAPTER 05

Your First Wife

Much has been written about the role your first wife plays in your journey to marry a second. It is worth repeating and ingraining within the depth of your very soul that this woman, whom you have classified as your soulmate, is the single most important person to consider while you navigate this complex equation called polygamy. Her life will never be the same again, something you can never afford to forget. Carved in stone within **your heart and mind** should be the realisation that your soulmate, from the day she knew you wished to marry another woman, believes deep within **her heart and mind** that she is losing something. Losing her best friend, her lover, her confidante, her companion, and everything she cherished with the man she also classified as her soulmate. It doesn't matter how much time you spend trying to convince her that she won't lose anything because coming from you at that moment will be ineffective and even patronising to her. It will hurt to the very core of her being, and she will feel completely inadequate and valueless, believing also that while something is being deducted from her life, more is added to yours without her participation. She will be contemplating deeply about how the love of her life wishes to be intimate with someone other than her, and when you stop to think how you would feel if it was the other way round, you can understand the magnitude of the gut-wrenching emotions she will be experiencing. True, men and women are wired differently, and we have written about this at some length, but put that aside for the moment and empathise with her desperate emotional plight caused by your actions alone.

Bearing all this in mind, navigating her emotions poses the biggest challenge and is something you cannot afford to take lightly. How you deal with informing her and the timing you choose to do so, or whether you decide not to inform her and have her find out, are part of myriad scenarios you may encounter. You need to make some tough decisions. Therefore, it is critical that you think carefully about how you plan to approach her with this news.

A Conversation About Polygamy

In a Muslim marriage, conversations about polygamy do crop up from time to time, initiated by either spouse, usually to test individual waters. Your aim could be to understand how your wife feels about it in general terms as an ideology and institution permissible in Islam, expecting her to accept it as such because, after all, she is a believing Muslim. At the same time, you closely observe her demeanour during these conversations to look for signs as to whether you think she, herself, could accept being in a polygamous relationship or not.

How will you know? Two possible scenarios:

• If she is silent about how she feels and gives you no overt clue, you must trust your instincts and in-depth knowledge of her personality by observing her expressions and demeanour. Is it something she is amenable to or something that she definitely **does not ever want you to do ... never ever?** Unlikely, you would conclude wrongly, but if you did miscalculate, that would be an error of colossal proportions, and 'stupidity' would likely have to be re-defined, especially for you.

• If, on the other hand, and this is the more likely scenario, she observes the direct approach and her lips articulate with crystal clarity, "Honey, if-you-marry-another-woman, you-lose-me!" and then you still decide to marry again, a ward in the local psychiatric institution would deservedly need to be named in your honour.

As for your wife, she will be one of two types:

• The first type is one who is convinced without even an iota of doubt that you, her loving, caring, handsome and wonderful husband, have absolutely no inclination or desire to take on a second wife. Little does she know.

• The second type is one who knows that if you could, you would. What she will be trying to establish, from your demeanour and behaviour, is whether you **would actually** do it.

So, the lesson here is not to be lulled into a false sense of security, believing your wife can accept the idea of you marrying again or be convinced to accept it. Even if the interaction went pretty positively and her demeanour during the discussions pleasantly surprised you, it's not a given. Either she's testing the waters with you, or she is merely acknowledging, as a believing Muslim woman, that polygamy is from the permissible things God has afforded to Muslim men. **But not her Muslim man!** Yes, in her heart and mind, she knows Islam allows it, and some couples practise polygamy successfully, but also firm in her heart and mind is the conviction that, while it works well for other people, **it won't work for her.** You love her; she knows that and banks on that knowledge to tell herself that you don't have and will never have any inclination to pursue the polygamy path. Unfortunately for her, she's wrong ... right?

So, the question remains, if you want to pursue this path, do you inform your wife, and when? Or do you not inform her, and under what circumstances? And when she finds out, what do you do? The following sections attempt to analyse various scenarios and offer suggestions on how to approach each in the most pragmatic way possible.

Should You Inform Her Of Your Intention To Marry?

YES!

Is that it? Indeed, it is. Laconic but also meant to convey a deeply profound and thought-provoking message to my fellow wannabe polygamists. It's the proverbial six-million-dollar question, which does not have a six-million-dollar answer. So, let me try to expand on this to give you some insight into a seemingly straightforward question, generating an answer that comes with inherent complications.

Option One – Informing Her Before

I mentioned at length what a first wife means to us as men. Most probably, they are the mothers of our children, our soulmates, and everything in the world to us. In a perfect world under perfect circumstances where your wife would be fully supportive of your desire to marry a second woman, the answer to this question would be an absolute and emphatic "YES." Why would it not be? If she was on board with the idea, you would basically and gleefully find yourself in a "polygamist" utopia where all things are bright and beautiful. Hunky-dory indeed, without a worry in the world. Heck, you could even marry more than two and probably not bat an eyelid.

The reality, of course, is quite different. Mind you, there are first wives who are completely supportive of their husbands' desires. I know, I have one and I have encountered a few others too. Rare and unique breeds of women, no doubt. Alas, sadly (for you), it's not **your** first wife that I am describing, so wake up from that blissful dream and smell the real coffee. Now, allow me to rephrase the question slightly and ask it this way: "If you know your wife will be quite devastated by the idea, should I tell her?" My answer is still an emphatic "YES", but with a few caveats, which I will come to later on.

Earnestly keep in mind and never forget that your first wife has earned sufficient respect through the many sacrifices she has made for you, some of which I have discussed previously. She knows you better and more intimately than anyone in the world, and hiding such an earth-shattering piece of information from her would be an insult to her dignity and a total lack of respect for her position in your life. Whatever fear or apprehension you may have of informing her of your desire, cast them aside and face her like the man you are. She may initially despise you for even thinking about the idea, but she will respect you for it when the dust settles in the not-too-distant future. Failing to tell her and then she finds out (and she will almost always find out), not from you, but through some gossip-mongering outlets, is a pure recipe for disaster, and you may as well then dig your grave, write your own obituary, and jump right in. The point to understand here is that the magnitude of that moment is like nothing you will experience in your life. Therefore, the more pragmatic and less calamitous approach would be to confide in your first wife, explaining why you need to do this and trust that your relationship is solid enough to withstand the ensuing storm.

• If She Asks Me, "Am I Not Enough?"

It is at this point that she may ask you the question, "Am I not enough?" A question conjoined with an animated look so melancholy that a facial emoticon could be replicated with it for social media memes. Do not weasel your way out of this awkward moment by saying something nonsensical like "Honey, you are enough, but bla bla bla……" Selling ice to an Eskimo would be a smarter thing to do. The reality and incontrovertible truth are that she is not enough physically, but not because she is inadequate as a person. You need to spend a lot of time and energy emphasising this point to her. It will be the most difficult part for her to digest, and this is where your understanding must be showcased uninhibited. Mess this moment up, and you will face an uphill battle to resume any semblance of normalcy in your relationship. So, be forthright and honest and say that it is the nature of men to want more than one woman, as well as all the rest of the philosophy I touched on earlier. In most instances, she, as a mature woman, will know this but may find it extremely difficult to swallow when she is directly affected. It will take time, but she will understand and accept it in due course.

Option Two – Informing Her After

One possible scenario would be to leave it until after the second marriage. It would constitute somewhat of the cowardice approach, but it may be warranted in a given circumstance. If you plan to do it this way, you had better be absolutely sure this approach has been thought through carefully, having calculated precisely and accurately that your first wife will react stoically and not go ballistic.

If your wife is not known for stoicism, and you still decide to go forward with a second marriage, informing her of what you did afterwards, be prepared for an avalanche of emotional abuse. The phrase 'shock and awe' will have a new meaning in your life. That fan in your bedroom will be soiled with you know what, and the spinning blades will unleash unending volumes of grief and misery upon you, affecting everyone around you, including the poor woman who accepted to be your second wife. All because you completely and utterly miscalculated your first wife's reaction, believing you knew her well but misreading this one miserably. And you know what? This is a self-inflicted wound and would be entirely your fault! You will now be faced with one of two options; either the staggeringly daunting task of convincing your first wife that this will all work out well – good luck with that! Or an ultimatum from her that is, "It's either me or her." Stuck between a rock and a hard place in a deep canyon with threatening rainstorms would be mentally more comforting.

So how do you get out of this "jail" with no "get-out-of-jail-free" cards? There is no easy answer for the two impossible choices you are faced with. Joint couple therapy, both personally and professionally, with third-party involvement, would probably be the best way forward. Be prepared for long interrogations with a series of intense questions starting with "How the heck did you miscalculate this?" Alternatively, if the idea of losing your first wife is real and impossible to stomach, and your relationship with your second wife has not blossomed into anything significant emotionally, then the most practically stable option would be to divorce your new wife and gift her something significant (not flowers) to help her get over the emotional trauma you inflicted on her. None of these options is ideal, and each situation is nuanced, but sometimes in life, you have got to examine all the horrible choices in front of you, then determine and choose the lesser of two evils and move on. And, of course, apologise profusely to all those whom you have detrimentally affected. Finally, do not allow yourself to make such an imbecilic mistake again. Take up voluntary fasting if you must curb your desires.

When Not To Tell Your Wife?

In the midst of what has been said on this subject and then to entertain the idea that there may actually be instances when men should refrain from telling their wives of their intention to re-marry sounds pretty sinister, to say the least. The audacity of such a notion stink of betrayal, injustice, and cruelty. I get that. But not everything in life is black and white. Nor is every situation and every relationship identical. So, exceptions do need to be understood and sometimes made.

I alluded previously to the immorality of illicit affairs and casual flings. Men do what men do and far be it for me to make a moral judgement on why. No one is perfect, and no one is immune to straying in some shape or form from the moral compass of certain values they have been brought up with and may uphold in their lives. Human beings have hypocritical tendencies to varying degrees, and it would be insincere not to acknowledge this as part of one's frailty. It does not necessarily make us bad people, but it does make us human, and to err is, after all, human.

That being said, we can say with conviction that a married man engaging in casual flings and illicit affairs is not a good thing, putting it very mildly. It is not something that is spoken about with pride and joy but rather with shame and disgrace. We can all agree here. So, where am I going with this?

Some men are simply addictively obsessed with women to such a degree that it is biologically impossible for them to stay faithful to one woman. They love their wives and families deeply yet have an insatiable addiction that surpasses any efforts they may have made to restrain themselves from their 'extra-curricular' activities. Do they need therapy? Probably, but many will not acknowledge their condition for fear of shame or ridicule. Sexual addiction is a 'thing', and societies, particularly conservative ones that attach a taboo to this addiction, need to rethink their position, acknowledge the reality and show empathy. People do suffer from such a condition and do require treatment so that they themselves and their societies at large are not detrimentally affected. Western liberal societies are more advanced in acknowledging the phenomenon, and others should follow suit for the general benefit of their members.

For religious men and, indeed, men who have been brought up with some religious values, this becomes a significant conundrum. Judeo-Christian and Islamic theology teaches that sexual misdemeanours committed through illicit arrangements are egregious wrongdoings with serious consequences in life after death. Those conscious of this injunction, yet having an insatiable yearning for physical intimacy, struggle in their lives, and hence, some of them are unable to observe restraint, thereby engaging in an activity that has serious spiritual consequences. Let me hasten to add that they are committing a sin and wrongdoing and are to be held responsible for their actions despite their nature. This is in no way an attempt to justify their misdemeanours or exonerate them from blame; however, like all human beings, they have their own weaknesses and struggles.

This lengthy preamble was necessary to set the context as to why, in certain circumstances, men may feel compelled to marry again without informing their first wife due to the fear of losing that cherished relationship he has established with her. This is more relevant when he is convinced that the idea of polygamy will be retaliated with fierce objection and threats of divorce. No man wants to lose his family. Furthermore, trying to garner sympathy for his desire to marry another woman because of his insatiable appetite would be an exercise in absolute futility, mocked and ridiculed by everyone and their pets.

If you are such a man living in a similar environment expecting fierce hostility if you choose to embark on the polygamy route, you will have to navigate this conundrum carefully and wisely, safeguarding your most cherished possessions, your religious values and your family. If you are convinced that the probability of your wife finding out is slim or next to nothing, you may wish to proceed with your desire unannounced out of fear of falling into something sinful. However, if you do not have such a conviction and the risk of losing your family will devastate you, then think very carefully before embarking on a possible suicide mission. My repeated advice for Muslim men, particularly when they face an impossible situation, is to observe voluntary fasting to curb their desires, seek therapy, if necessary, and learn to appreciate what you do have giving up on your dream for that 'half hour of extra entertainment.' The bigger picture is more critical for you.

• *True Story*

Several years ago, I was approached by a friend of mine who asked me to counsel two young married men who were seriously exploring polygamy as a lifestyle. They were successful businessmen who travelled the region for their businesses. Initially, I was not sure how I could help them (I did not have that much experience). However, I agreed to meet with them, and while we sat for some tea, we discussed the idea. They were determined to embark on the polygamy journey for reasons obvious to all at that meeting. They were coming from a conservative background, so I asked a few questions. Are you financially capable of looking after a second wife? Will you inform your first wife? Both answered "yes" and "no", respectively. Then I asked if there was any possibility that your first wife would find out. "Yes, the possibility exists," they responded. So, I pursued my line of questioning and asked them, if she does find out, what do you expect her reaction to be? Almost simultaneously and with full conviction, they said, "She will divorce me." Finally, I asked them, if their wives were to divorce them, would this be something that would affect them and their lives detrimentally? Surprisingly, one of them responded that this would not bother him, and his wife would be free to leave the marriage. The other was the complete opposite. He confessed that he would be deeply affected and devastated. So, to the first young man with the nonchalant "I don't really care" answer, I remarked (also with nonchalance) that there is no real need for me to counsel him since there is nothing I can say if he has no real concern for his first wife's feelings. (If his wife did find out and divorced him, he'd end up having only one wife, effectively defeating the whole purpose of his mission to be married to two women. Obviously, he didn't think it through). To the second gentleman, I advised him to think very carefully about how he conducts himself because, in his situation, if he ended up losing his first wife (and family – he had a young child at that time), he would likely lose everything he had built to that day. He would not achieve happiness even if he were to marry again. I never met them after that encounter, so I never found out how they faired.

When Your First Wife Finds Out

If you choose the risky and clandestine approach in finding a second wife, do so with the knowledge and belief that your first wife will almost definitely find out at some point. Do not, I repeat, DO NOT fool yourself into thinking that you have a foolproof plan and that your actions will never come to light and be discovered. You do so at your own psychological peril. Particularly, if you marry someone in the same city that you live and work in, there's a good chance you're going to meet your first wife's best friend in the mall while you are with your second wife, and she will tell her what she saw; your clothes will smell of unfamiliar perfume; your pockets will be stuffed with restaurant receipts to a restaurant you never took your first wife to, and the worst of all scenarios – when, during a romantic moment with your first wife you tell her "I love you so much, Khadija!" and her name is Ayesha! Ouch! If that happens while you are in the kitchen and you see a frying pan, use it on your head.

So, what to do? The same need for patience, maturity and understanding if you were to tell your wife beforehand is required, served with more patience, maturity and understanding. Because the situation is graver. Also, the ability to keep your tongue in check from quipping anything remotely sarcastic and/or idiotic will help.

Armed with these traits, and in the virtually inevitable event that your first wife does find out, you can do one of two things. Face the apocalyptic next few days with all those virtuous traits or run. Obviously, I'm not serious; don't do that. Running will only demonstrate that you are a gutless coward on two counts; firstly, that you didn't have the courage to tell her in advance, and secondly, when she did find out, you chickened out from your responsibilities. You decided to go incognito, believing that the 'half an hour of extra entertainment' was worth this, so now you need to face what will feel like a domestic Armageddon in your home, all because of the decisions you made.

What reaction should you expect? Each person reacts in different ways but usually expect to receive either a tsunami of abuse; or an eerie and mentally excruciating silence for several hours, days or even weeks. You choose which one is worse. If you had been married for a significantly longer period and established a tight bond between the two of you, the hurt would be monumental and catastrophic, and the reaction equally commensurate. You must recognise this and allow her whatever space she wants. And if she does not want space, you have got to be there to deal with her reaction. Pray that your second wife is an understanding woman and can allow you the time away from her for a short while.

It may be hard to believe at that moment, but here again trust me when I say the dust will settle. It always settles and how soon will largely depend on the way you deal with the initial reaction. At this point, you must force a calm and collected dialogue explaining why you had to do this in this way, how you didn't want to lose her or your family, and at any cost, how deeply committed you are to them. Shower her with gifts and a short holiday if you are able, as I suggested earlier. Again, it's not a bribe. Make her feel that she is the love of your life without making any corny verbal claims at that moment, like "You are the love of my life!" At that moment it just won't fly, but her fist may, in the direction of your face.

Takeaway

The takeaway from this section is to be forthright in your intentions and your actions when those actions are going to affect the people closest to you, and there is no one closer than your wife. For first-time polygamists, you will be faced with very delicate surroundings, and it is critical that you are aware that you must act maturely and sensitively. You can certainly allow yourself the freedom to feel guilt-free for something you really need to do, without ignoring the sensitivities of your family, who may not quite understand what all the fuss is about and why you cannot be satisfied with what you already have. And when the crisis hits, do not exacerbate the situation by acting in ways that worsen the crisis. Pomp, arrogance, and insensitivity are the perfect recipe for a suicide mission leading to divorce and destruction of family.

CHAPTER 06

The Aftermath

For those of you who have reached this exclusive – and indeed elusive – milestone, and you now have two wives, let's be upbeat and positive. I offer you a hearty congratulations. You persevered, showcasing your patience and fortitude against many odds, and you are now where you want to be. Your family has gone through a lot, too, for you to reach where you are. Empathy, however, would naturally be leaning heavily on the side of those affected by your actions, and not so much with you (or should I say **not at all** with you), yet the mental strain that you endured cannot be ignored, even if it was never recognised. Most likely, and most unfortunately, you will be forced to deal with any detrimental effects on your mental health by yourself. This is where your second wife may play a crucial role in helping you, so I hope that you have chosen wisely. If, however, in the aftermath of your second marriage, you find yourself emotionally alone, then please talk to someone or think about attending useful therapy sessions. I discuss this in a little more detail later.

The New Normal

It will need a little getting used to, but you are now living a lifestyle strikingly different from what you had led up to this moment. Not only do you have an additional person to physically attend to, but you will also be required to emotionally deal with all the "others" that have been affected. Believe me when I say that the emotional management you will be compelled to navigate will be much more complicated than the physical journeys (obliged upon you as a proud man with two wives) to and from the different households each night. No two women are the same, and no two households are the same. If you have been married to your first wife for a substantial period, this new normal where you will be encountering a different personality, possibly every other night, can be daunting. With your first wife, you are accustomed to a particular routine and a distinct personality with whom you have an intimate understanding and familiarity. You are familiar with the way she addresses you, the way she cooks for you, the way she appears in front of you, and even extends to the way you prefer to appear in front of her.

It is a highly nuanced situation when you are dealing with two different personalities. If you find a second wife who resembles your first one in terms of personality, your early days of polygamy will not bring with it too many surprises. You may not have to modify your behaviour drastically to navigate the process of dealing with your new normal. However, it is also very possible that you will be faced with a completely different personality to deal with, for better or worse, and it may take a little while in the relationship for it to dawn on you. You don't really know someone until you live with them. When that happens, stop, take a step back and find a formula to revamp the way you manage this new entry in your life. This will necessarily involve altering some aspects of your demeanour and behaviour to accommodate her personality and there is nothing schizophrenic or hypocritical about this modification. We do it all the time in other facets of our life. You don't behave the same way with your boss as you do with your subordinates or with your father the same way you do with your son. Compare how you behave (or misbehave) in a football match where your favourite team is playing the finals of an important tournament with an evening business dinner you attend, hosting important dignitaries or clients. We adapt, and we acclimatise to our environment, and it is not too dissimilar in a polygamous relationship when dealing with the new and different personality who is now your second wife.

Managing Jealousy Effectively

Jealousy is an emotion that cuts across all genders and situations. Jealousy exists among siblings, children, co-workers, and the list can go on. The jealousy between two wives, however, is a next-level phenomenon. If you don't recognise this and are not prepared to deal with it, turmoil and grief will likely be your new status quo. Jealousy will either surface intrinsically or by manufacture. Intrinsic jealousy is beyond your immediate control because it surfaces as a natural consequence of your decision to marry again. Most likely, you will see this more in your first wife than in your second. Reassure her of your love and commitment to her, spend quality time with her, and shower her with gifts she will value over a lifetime. Gradually, her jealousy will simmer down and reach a level close to non-existent.

Jealousy manufactured, on the other hand, is a consequence of your actions and behaviour. The next section on navigating between two personalities suggests some ways to combat this phenomenon.

Navigating Between Two Personalities

In the previous section, we touched on the notion that being in a polygamous relationship requires little mental gymnastics to navigate between two (or more) personalities. Physically, it requires you to also do certain things and not do other things that could jeopardise any balance or status quo you may have worked hard to achieve. I cannot overstate the importance of fine-tuning this skill, nor can you underestimate the need to take it seriously. Like any new adventure, you face uncertainties and the need to go through trial and error before mastering its art. In a relationship of this nature, you may have some time for trial but very little time for errors. Some errors are worse than others, and you won't know that until you make them, at which point you may be saying "au revoir" to one or the other of your wives or, God forbid, both.

Dos And Don'ts With Wives

Dos and don'ts are essentially rules of behaviour that need to be adhered to. Here are a few. Although the list can never be exhaustive, it may save you much grief during the polygamy journey and enable it to last a lifetime In Sha Allah.

• Do - Identify Their Distinct Personalities

Do this quickly because time is short. Despite some general similarities, every woman has her own distinct personality, ranging from mild at one end of the spectrum to strong and, dare I say, aggressive at the other. And before I am lambasted for focusing on women, let me hasten to add that men are the same, and I will go further and concede, more dangerously so. Someone once said, "You can change someone's habits, but not their nature", and the sooner you realise this, the sweeter and less traumatic your life will be. Understanding each one and contrasting their personalities will help you immensely in dealing with their differences in an effective way wisely.

• Do – Keep Your Ego In Check

Men are egotistical by nature -- many women would agree and want to add the word "pigs" for emphasis. We do have our fair share of nutters within the male species, and I do apologize on their behalf. But there are good men out there, too. Having an ego in and of itself is not something that is inherently bad, except when it makes you do bad stuff bordering on verbal and physical abuse and then actually reaching such pathetic levels. This could happen to strong-willed, hot-tempered men and, in particular, those who have been accustomed to one type of personality for a long time and are then faced with someone who is a little different and perhaps more demanding. The key here is twofold. Firstly, to understand where this personality stems from and the kind of upbringing and history that fostered it, and then exercise patience and wisdom in dealing with the unfamiliarity of it all. Easy right? Secondly, if indeed you do have an anger management problem, go seek help now. You are a danger to yourself, to your new wife and anyone in close proximity.

• *Do – Treat Them Equally And Fairly*

It is a religious obligation and a moral one to always be equal between your wives, not only in terms of finances but also in terms of your time and your treatment of them. Financial equality here refers to gifts, travelling on vacations and the like, whether either of them knows about what you do for the other or not. As far as time is concerned, you need to figure out a formula with your wives for how this will work and come to a mutually acceptable arrangement. Perhaps alternating between each household daily or more than that, but importantly, with equality and consistency. And if you ever have them in the same room together, treating them the same is probably the most important. If they smell a hint of inequality, this will not go well for you.

• *Do – Compliment Them Regularly*

Everyone likes to be complimented, and in particular, women from their husbands. Get into the habit of regularly using many complementary words and phrases in the homes of your wives. Be consistent in doing this for all your wives so that it becomes almost second nature to you and observe the sparkle in their eyes. Regardless of their individual personalities, sincere compliments are essential in setting the right ambience for the rest of the evening with the wife you are staying with that day. Avoid complimenting either wife in front of the other as it will get complicated when you are encountered with a question like, for example, "Why did you say she is a patient person? Are you saying I'm not?"

• *Don't – Compare Them With Each Other*

If there was a cardinal sin in navigating a polygamous relationship, this one would certainly be vying for the top spot. We have billions of brain cells, but only one is required to know that you do not say to either wife, for example, "She cooks better than you" or "Her house is kept cleaner than yours," and probably the most dim-witted one, "I think she is more beautiful than you". If you do this, perhaps in a state of anger or temporary insanity, I hope you have a comfortable sofa in your home. On a serious note, in whatever dysfunctional state of anger you happen to be in, **restrain yourself from making any direct or even indirect comparisons** whatsoever. For example, if you don't help wash dishes in one household, take the laundry out, or help with the cooking, don't say to the occupant of one that you do or did so in the household of the other. Volunteering such information is unnecessary and honestly foolish. There are many examples, but hopefully, you get the gist.

• *Who Is More Beloved?*

A particular issue, and quite probably a contentious one I would like to specifically address, is a question that one or both of your wives may ask you at some point, either in a serious and poignant moment between yourselves or in a moment of jest (which is usually her way of testing you). The question is, "Whom do you love more?" Now, if you are recently married to the second woman who asks you this question, you may be tempted to think, and naturally so, that she would understand if you told her that you loved your first wife more. Well, in most circumstances, you would be dead wrong. I personally do not advocate lying under almost any circumstances, except in this case, if you suspect strongly in advance, the reaction would be a ballistic one. So, based on my experience; to keep the discussion short, you can tell her that it is she you love more. The same, of course, applies to the first wife.

However, another more pragmatic approach is to turn the question around and say to her that it is not really relevant to her who you love more, but what is relevant is the manner in which you are treating her to earn love and respect. It's not possible that a human heart can be demarcated and mathematically apportioned love to different people, let alone wives. When you love, you love ... but how you exemplify that love is key. By saying this, you have not put your foot in your mouth if the other wife ever discovers you said what you said. And for the wise woman, this answer is sufficient because it makes complete sense.

• Don't – Confuse Their Names

Another competitor for the top spot in cardinal sin gaffes. You may believe this would never happen, and you may even believe that if it did, it would be no big deal. Wrong! It can very easily, even if inadvertently so, happen, and it will be a big deal, especially if it happens in a moment of intimacy. Have your cold shower ready. So, be always on your mental guard, particularly if you are "fortunate" enough to have more than two.

Takeaway

The main takeaway from this section is to understand the mental and psychological challenges you will face in the new lifestyle you have created for yourself and deal with the different personalities of your wives while navigating this lifestyle. Theoretically, understanding what you should and should not do is relatively simple, but putting that into practice is a completely different ballgame altogether. Many of these challenges you are faced with may indeed be beyond your control; however, your success in dealing with them will depend on how sophisticated you are in your ability to look at the big picture. That big picture is your happiness and mental health and of those around you and directly affected by your actions. As for matters within your control, like ego, equality, and treatment, it is imperative that you strive and make concerted efforts each and every day to be responsible, think maturely and maintain justice between your spouses. Keep reminding yourself regularly that ***it is not only*** about that 'half an hour of extra entertainment' each night.

CHAPTER 07

Your Second Wife

I have casually referred to the second wife at certain points in various contexts where a man is considering, then looking for and finally entering into a marriage with another woman. However, casual references do absolutely no justice to her and her importance in this complex polygamy equation. In the beginning, when you are thinking about a second wife, your first wife and her feelings would naturally have to be your priority and sole focus. While there is never a moment where you should ever reduce your concern for your first wife and her emotional well-being - remember, dude, you're the reason for her trauma - the focus can no longer be one-dimensional once you marry number two. In this chapter, I would like to share more insights on how to navigate the process of establishing a solid foundation and happy relationship with the other woman you have invited to share your life with.

Choosing Wisely

It all starts here. If there was a list of, shall we say, "Ten Commandments" in the world of polygamy, then choosing the right woman to be your second wife would, without doubt, be at the top of that sacred list? I drew a cheeky parallel earlier when I said that in the context of men's obsession with and desire for women, marrying multiple women is like ordering and trying different foods. That's where the parallel ends. You can always return a culinary dish if you don't like it. So, let's explore some of the factors that come into play when you meet a potential candidate and decide whether or not to proceed.

• *Physical Attraction*

It is naturally tempting to focus on physical beauty when considering someone to be your new wife, and it is absolutely not an unimportant factor in the decision-making process. Men will always be men, and physical beauty is commonly the first characteristic that we look for in our partners in life. Physical beauty is largely objective and often clear-cut but can also be subjective, with different people having their own preferences. Personally, I strongly advocate that your attraction to the lady you are considering marrying is equal to or greater than your attraction to your first wife. Sounds inconsiderate and even mean-spirited, but it really is not. Unless you tell your first wife that you found someone more attractive, and you would not do that obviously because you are not that stupid. Or are you?

If you rush into the choice, overlooking your preferences in terms of physical attraction, you may initially be overwhelmed with the exuberance of having someone other than your wife to experience intimacy with. Trust me, it won't last. New brooms do sweep well, but you will not be able to sustain that high for long.

Be wary of women who look appealing with makeup on but are average with it off. Here again, there is a level of subjectivity, and based on your own preferences, you should immediately conclude whether you can sustain that attraction or not. If you rush into the marriage prematurely and later discover the attraction is not sustainable, you risk devastating the life of the poor lady you married as your second wife for the selfish choice you made just to satisfy your libido. That would be quite pathetic, so please stop yourself, be patient and wait for the right one to come. She will come.

• Another True Story

When I began the journey, the very first instance where I encountered the possibility of exploring an actual marriage potential was when I was asked by someone if I would be interested in considering marrying a lady he is acquainted with. Instinctively, I asked him if I could see what she looked like, and he suggested that I walk across to her place of work and introduce myself. This suggestion wasn't really appealing to me, so instead, I counter-proposed that I visit her place of work, walk by her desk, and if I saw a potential in terms of a physical attraction, then and only then, we can discuss introductions. He agreed, and I did exactly that. I realised immediately that there was no physical attraction and, therefore, no possibility that I could do any kind of justice in a marriage with this particular lady. I informed him of my decision and left it at that, and the lady knew nothing about what we discussed and planned when I visited her workplace. It happened exactly how I wanted it to because it is not nice to be told that you are not attractive to someone. Fast forward one year, and this same acquaintance informed me that he has plans to marry her. He was already married, and while congratulating him, I asked him if he was sure he could pull this off from the perspective of his first wife's sentiments – in other words, her acceptance when he informs her because he was planning to tell her after the wedding. I also asked him subtly if he was physically attracted to his new wife-to-be and able to sustain this attraction throughout his married life. He assured me on both fronts and proceeded with the marriage. Another fast forward, and in two months, not only had he completely miscalculated his first wife's acceptance, but also "remarkably" – and annoyingly to me - miscalculated his level of physical attraction to his new wife. Stuck in a crevice with flesh-eating ants would have been simpler for him to deal with, and unfortunately, he made the choice to divorce his new wife abruptly. This poor lady, now devastated, had no recourse except to the financial promises stipulated in the original marriage contract in the event of him divorcing her.

The lesson to learn here is obvious.

Ideological Affinity

If you are a person who has very strong opinions on humankind, life, religion, and the universe, married life would be extremely straightforward if your second wife-to-be shares the same effervescence for such diverse and possibly controversial world views. A relationship with a woman who is as strongly opinionated as you are (and there is nothing wrong with that) but has an opposite or contrasting worldview could potentially climax into a vitriolic bloodbath (figuratively speaking), rendering reconciliation futile. I also want to make the point that it is not about which worldview is correct. Each is entitled to what they believe and live by. It is about maintaining harmony in the home. So, it would be perfectly okay to discuss such issues in advance before making any marriage commitment, and if the ideological differences are stark and insurmountable, it would also be perfectly okay to say "thanks, but no thanks."

Warning! Do not allow yourself to be awestruck by someone you may find exceptionally beautiful yet still possess ideological opinions and views starkly contrasting to yours. The awe will vanish once the battle of ideologies turns nasty.

Cultural Affinity

The beautiful world we live in is home to people of so many different nationalities and diverse cultural backgrounds. Appreciating these different cultures from afar and even partaking in them from time to time provides us with rich and meaningful exposures that will surely enhance our life experiences. Marrying into these cultures, however, is not always so straightforward. Each culture comes with its idiosyncrasies – not necessarily good or bad, but different – and people familiar with and accustomed to these idiosyncratic tendencies usually function much better in that environment. If you find a second wife who shares the same cultural background, adjusting your existing lifestyle is far less tedious than when she is coming from a completely different one. Things like preferences for food, enjoying recreation and entertainment, dealing with family members, managing finances and the home, and even issues as mundane as "How many times do you need to brush your teeth in the morning?" or "Do you need to make so much noise while you are eating?" can be sticking points to overcome.

This is not to say that being in a polygamous relationship with someone from a different culture is doomed to fail. Heck no, it can be very rewarding, but realise that respect and understanding are paramount in adjusting to and accepting patterns of behaviour different from yours. When you do that, you taste the sweet variety of life and the lifestyle you have chosen.

Informing Her You Are Married

Early in the process of meeting and choosing someone suitable to be your second wife, you need to inform her that you are also a happily married man. This is a vital piece of information, and it is imperative, in my opinion and experience, that she is aware of this at the very outset. This way, she has the choice to accept you or not without having invested any time, energy, or emotion. Keeping this information from her for later is not a wise idea because it puts her at a significant disadvantage in the decision-making process. Moreover, it could be a deal breaker at a time when both of you have invested significantly. It's like, for example, she keeps the information about her three children, an elderly mother suffering from Alzheimer's, and a paralyzed bedridden father from you, and then on your honeymoon springs a surprise: "Honey, by the way, I forgot to mention, guess who's going to be living with us?" Well, not quite, but you get the point. At such an important milestone in your life, each of you must be given every piece of relevant information that will contribute to the decision-making process. You *are* married to another woman, and that *is* relevant.

Having Children

One issue that you will most likely have to address when you consider entering into a second marriage is that of children. Nothing to do with your own or her own children, and I cover some aspects of this in a later chapter. Rather, it has to do with whether you and/or your new intended spouse want to share the experience of having a child together.

If you are a man looking to marry another woman because you want more children, and there are plenty of men like you, the issue is less contentious if your new wife shares the same feelings. If she doesn't and this is a deal breaker for you, you need to be upfront from the outset before too much has been invested in the relationship.

If you are not looking to have children with your second wife, and she shares the same sentiment, then all is fine and dandy. But if she does not share the same views, again, you would need to be upfront with her and move on with your life, finding someone who is compatible with your position. If, on the other hand, you believe that she is truly the one and everything about her checks most of your boxes, then you need to navigate this difference pragmatically, and especially for Muslim men within the Islamic faith, which encourages procreation. Remove the fear of having children and place your trust in God as a believing Muslim, believing that He is the ultimate Provider of sustenance and that the blessing of a child with the one you love is one of His most beautiful gifts.

The New Family Member

For so long now, you have been accustomed to referring to your first wife and kids (if you have any) as your "family". Once you have embraced another woman into your life as a wife, she also becomes a member of your family, and it is vitally important that she is made to feel that way immediately. You can do this in a very direct way by saying something like "welcome to the family" and other words of endearment to give her the confidence that you do think she deserves that place. You can and must do so in indirect ways, as well, by treating her no differently than you would your first family in terms of words and deeds. Which is why we emphasized equality when giving gifts, good treatment and the like.

Bear in mind that she is most likely coming into an environment that she is completely unfamiliar with. She may or may not know the struggles and intensities that you and your family experienced in arriving at the place where she has become your new wife. She will live her married life with you, at least during the early stages, with uncertainties about any possible hostility she may face from other family members, making her feel unwanted. She could be afraid of your first wife and feel like she is encroaching and upsetting the status quo you had before. No one likes to feel like a third wheel, and it is your job to quell her insecurities with a lot of respect, affection, and time.

Showing Respect

Respect is something any human being desires and deserves, and your new wife is no less. Respecting her, however, takes on a different look, which addresses some of the nuances of her specific situation. Some ways of showing respect are explained below:

• She may be your second wife chronologically, but never refer to her or introduce her as your "second wife". You should refer to or introduce her as "your wife."

• Always make her feel that she is your only wife in private.

• Don't make patronising references to your first wife in any conversation with your second, even during an argument.

• Don't mention any gift you may have given your first wife if you do not plan to do the same for her. The same applies to recreational activities like vacations, picnics and similar. (Mind you, being equal is a religious obligation on you, so this should never happen under any circumstances anyway)

• Being condescending is bad enough, but doing so in front of your first wife and family is torturous for your second. Restrain yourself with all your might and effort if you must.

• Keep your arguments private and strictly avoid seeking counsel from your first wife in any dispute you have with your second. And vice versa. Unless, of course, there is an all-around understanding and agreement, and the relationship between your wives is amicable.

• Always make her feel secure in the marriage and avoid even innocuous threats of divorce in the heat of any argument.

Displaying Affection

Overt displays of sincere affection towards your wives are always welcome, but obviously not in front of each other where possible. Hugging your wife often (apparently releases endorphins from her body, lowers cortisol, the stress hormone, and produces scientifically concluded benefits) is the obvious way of displaying affection that will give her a sense of security; words may not always do. It's free, so don't be stingy with it.

Spending Time With Her

Kind words, gifts, and physical affection are always endearing, but nothing can truly replace the time you give your wives, particularly a newly wedded one. Here, I am referring to quality time. Not time spent individually and indifferently on opposite sides of the same enclosure scrolling social media platforms. To make matters worse, you then burst into sudden and probably idiotic laughter because of something on TikTok that you found funny. Not cool! I am stating the obvious, but apparently, the obvious needs to be stated and sometimes drilled into many insensitive men.

Separate Households, Homes, & Lives

When you marry for the second time, I mentioned previously how maintaining a separate physical household is something obligatory upon you and a religious right of your wives. What this also means is "home", that sanctuary where you go to find peace and tranquillity, now becomes two different physical residences with two different persons living in each of them. And consequently, it will also mean that you are living two separate lives and all the baggage that comes with it. Without a doubt, it is a huge transition that will take some getting used to for you and for your family, but it is an important psychological one you (and your first and, indeed, second wife and family) are compelled to embrace. You didn't think of all of this when you wanted that half-hour extra entertainment, did you?

Part of nurturing the relationship with your new wife is also allowing her the space to make a home for you without any of the baggage that comes with your first family. I spoke about the importance of navigating between two personalities earlier, and this skill will be tested to its core when you navigate between two homes. Your new wife will want to do things her way, and you must be open to her preferences, support her efforts to make you happy and make this relationship work while exhibiting sincere joy that she is adding quality to your life, because she is.

Certain idiosyncrasies that you may witness in your new home may appear strange and unfamiliar to you and tempt you to reject them altogether. Before you rush to do that, think it over and form a conclusion for yourself as to whether or not you are inconvenienced by these unfamiliar habits and manners. If you are not, **do not hurt** the sensitivities of your new wife over something that is so minor. And if you **are** inconvenienced by them, again **do not hurt** the sensitivities of your new wife over something that is so minor. Accept them and move on.

Introducing Her To Your Wife And Family

The idea of your wives meeting each other and being friends is almost a utopian one for most polygamy practitioners. It does happen, and it's a beautiful thing to experience when it does but keep your own expectations very low. It probably will not happen for you. Nevertheless, it is highly likely that at some point in time, you will be forced to introduce them to each other, possibly under casual and inevitable circumstances. Likely a very awkward moment, which again will test your mental and even verbal navigation skills, and you will have to showcase that talent without messing it up by saying anything insensitive or foolish. As long as they are civil towards each other, the tension can be managed.

Is One Big Happy Family Possible?

Some men who embark on the path of polygamy do so with an idealistic vision and dream that once they marry their second wife, together with their first wife and family, they will all embrace this new normal wholeheartedly and become one big happy family. If you are such a man, you may dream of dining out often together, inviting each other regularly to their respective homes – maybe even pyjama parties – exchanging gifts at every possible opportunity, travelling on holidays together, and that cloud nine feeling of walking hand in hand with glee and pride written all over your face while showcasing your "trophies". You then wake up from this dream with a sudden and unpleasant jolt. Reality is different and that one big happy family vision will not happen, even if your wives are friends and civil with each other. I wouldn't say it could never evolve into such a state, but at the early stages of your journey, it is highly unlikely.

In truth, such a situation has more problems than benefits despite it being your avenue for psychological comfort, or so you thought. I would not spend too much time detailing all the possible drawbacks in such an arrangement, except to say that once the lifestyle is in place and you are living it day in and day out, it would be very difficult for either of your wives to be subjected to each other's presence constantly and persistently. We all know and have experienced that constant in-your-face feeling in a relationship, be it romantic or otherwise. And we all know it can be tedious and mentally straining. So be happy if they are at least civil with each other and consider that in itself to be a huge blessing.

Takeaway

The main takeaway from this section is to maintain your dignity and respect in how you treat your new wife and help her deal with a new life, new people, and new environment. An environment that may be, at best, uneasy and, at worst, hostile. Don't aggravate her fears by rejecting what she brings to the relationship because you are unaccustomed to the new personality. Also, be realistic and not too idealistic with your expectations, but at the same time, don't give up trying to reach for the stars. Nothing stays the same forever, and given time, what you thought was impossible to achieve may actually be around the corner.

CHAPTER 08

What About The
Children?

What about them? Isn't it really none of their business what goes on between you and your wife? Since when do you need your kids' permission to do what you wish to do in your life?

On the contrary, these are valid and important questions that may invade your mind as you pursue the lifestyle or if you are already in it. How you address them will depend on the relationship you have with your kids, how close or not you are to them, and, importantly, their ages and religious upbringing – particularly if they are Muslims.

How Close Are You To Them?

If your relationship with them is one of indifference and you are not close, then it really won't matter what they think, and they, too, would likely exhibit that indifference when you do what you have to do. "We hardly see Dad, so nothing really changes", is what they are probably going to think. Informing or not informing them makes no difference, and while this is a sad state of affairs, it does pave the way for your escapade into the lifestyle a little more easily.

If, on the other hand, you maintain a close relationship with your children and are actively involved in their lives, the situation becomes a little more delicate. I recall having a conversation with a close friend of mine who aspired to marry a second wife but did not have the courage to do so. He said to me, "My daughter would never speak to me if I married another woman."

Personally, I believe kids are able to adapt to changes much more effectively than adults. While my friend's daughter may feel contempt towards him initially, this will not remain forever, particularly if he adheres to the commitment mentioned previously about maintaining the same levels of interaction, love, and affection. Of course, deeds more than words will convince them that what you say is not merely paying lip service.

Their Age

How you deal with your kids will differ depending on their ages. Obviously, if they are infants or toddlers at an age where they are unable to discern the intricacies of what is happening in your life, the effect on them will be minimal, if not zero. They are your kids, though, and they will notice your absence when it is significant, so take care of that and ensure they are not neglected. They need to see and feel "daddy".

Young children and early teenagers are different, and their reactions will depend a lot on how they see their mother react, how you behave with her in general, and how you conduct yourself while pursuing the polygamy lifestyle. I have made it clear in this book and have earnestly insisted that you should always maintain dignity in how you conduct yourself and how you approach those affected by your actions. The dignified approach will rub off positively on your children, whereas the undignified approach will not. Simple as that.

As for adult children, your approach should be one of dialogue, consultation, and explanation, not necessarily for the purpose of seeking permission. Ultimately, you will do what you must do, but you do want them on your camp, if not wholeheartedly, at least non-objectionably. Mature and respectful discourse on a subject this contentious at such a personal level will garner you much more respect than if you displayed indifference to their views and emotions. You'll always be "dad", and they will always defend you to the core, even if they are not too thrilled with what you plan to do.

Their Religious Upbringing

The issue of polygamy remains one that is still quite taboo in Muslim societies, and we discussed earlier what is driving this objection, despite Muslims generally accepting wholeheartedly that it is an allowance from God. When it comes to your children and this subject, one of the methods you can adopt is to implant in them from an early age the notion that there is nothing criminal or illicit about polygamy and that it is impossible for God Almighty to legislate an allowance for something that is criminal or illicit. They may need further understanding of the rationale behind this legislation to cement their conviction. This is not too difficult to do, considering there is much material available to rationalise and justify the practice; and your guidance will also help.

If you had not implanted the justification at a young age, there is still hope that you can do so at a later stage. As young adults, they can be made to understand its rationale and why you want to practise this lifestyle.

Stepchildren

It is also possible that your second wife has a child or has children of her own from a previous marriage or marriages. They could be infants, youngsters, or even young adults. You should definitely be aware of their existence when you choose to pursue this lady as your wife. And if you genuinely did not know about them, you certainly have a huge bone to pick with her. Fundamentally, however, they are not your responsibility, and you should never be made to feel that they are. However, if they do not have any male role model in their lives to take charge of them, particularly if they are within an age range that requires such a person, I would highly recommend you be that person if, of course, you are able to do so without neglecting your obligations to other family members who have more of this right. What this will do is change the dynamics of how you are perceived by your second wife and her children because you were magnanimous enough to accept responsibility for persons for whom you have no obligations.

That is the epitome of generosity, and it's also spiritually rewarding. If you do have the means to provide for them and choose not to, you may not be blameworthy technically, but it will not come across well and potentially foster negative feelings and vibes in their hearts for a long time. This will not help your goal to achieve happiness and tranquillity in your marriage. So, please be generous.

Takeaway

The main takeaway from this section is to realise that your kids may be affected in one way or the other. You cannot ignore them, but you can do much to remove any negative emotions that may be simmering inside them. Importantly, and I mentioned this before, they must be made to understand that you are leading your life in the way you see fit, responsibly, while assuring them of your love and commitment to them and that your relationship with them will never be compromised, ever.

CHAPTER 09

Should A Wife Accept Polygamy?

"Why should she?" the antagonists will ask, and it is a reasonable question. The protagonist will, on the other hand, frame it like "Why she should?" and there is also merit in such a framing.

There is no easy answer to this question because of how emotive the issue is. Different societies have different values and customs, and where polygamy is practised relatively freely, the answer is not so contentious.

However, in societies that promote secular liberalism and gender equality, where the idea of marriage between one man and one woman has been instilled among its members as a de facto norm, the question has complexities attached to it. Trying to make sense using the modern-day lenses of an institution that required no rational explanation during its pre-modern evolution is challenging. The answers that do not fall in line with liberal values will be subject to critical scrutiny, and those advocating the rationale for polygamy may possibly be ridiculed and even castigated. However, Muslims who are confident in their beliefs and sufficiently knowledgeable about the jurisprudential ruling on the subject and its rationale, will be well placed to articulate responses to deal with these criticisms. They understand that modern-day values and morals are not carved in stone as necessarily superior just because many loud voices propagate its tenets. So, to help that cause to a certain degree, let us explore some of the answers to both the questions posed by the antagonist and protagonist trying to make rational sense – particularly to believing Muslim women – of a topic that brings out the fire in the belly in many.

God Almighty Permitted It

Most Muslims across the world will theoretically accept unconditionally the laws of God when He legislates certain regulations for humans. Practically applying some of those laws, however, is another thing and can sometimes be a challenge for even the most religious people. I promised this was not going to be a religious book, but what I want to do is to set the context for what comes next.

For Muslim women, the question of polygamy poses a difficult conundrum in terms of balancing their religious convictions with their emotions, and it is a hard one to navigate. Here, I need to clearly emphasise that, by no means does this make her deficient in her faith, and it should never be used as a kind of trump card to emotionally blackmail her into the polygamy lifestyle. It just means she is human and, like all of us, struggles with her desires and emotions when faced with some of the spiritual injunctions, commands, and prohibitions legislated by our Lord. Take, for example, Muslim men who choose a path of infidelity (which polygamy is not) while knowing and believing that such a path is strictly prohibited and an egregious transgression. I would argue that they do so because their spiritual struggle is significantly more calamitous, considering they actually fall into the sin of infidelity. The Muslim woman is not falling into any sin whatsoever simply because she finds it impossible to share her husband with another woman, so there is no moral equivalency between the two, and her faith should never be questioned because of her objection.

To my Muslim sister, if you are faced with a situation where your husband has made a concrete decision to marry another woman, and you are struggling big time with the prospect of sharing him, take comfort from a few things:

• God Almighty will never put you in a situation that is detrimental to you except that it is a means to raise your rank in His eyes.

• The world we live in is temporary, whereas the life after is eternal. The sacrifices you made for God's sake in this relatively short sojourn on earth will be compensated in multiples when you meet Him on the

Day of Judgement.

• The ability to want good for others as much as you want good for yourself is elevating your spirituality to the next level and cementing your position as a true believer in God. Paradise awaits you, In Sha Allah.

There is nothing I said that you do not already know, but reminding does profit the believers.

Inability To Satisfy Her Husband's Desires

It may be very true that some husbands are not physically satisfied with their wives, and their wives are unable to bring themselves to the level where they could be. And as true as that may be, it would also be deemed – by antagonists - a preposterous rationale for the argument in favour of accepting polygamy. "Why can't he control his desires?" is the expected and curt response. Why does the poor wife have to suffer for "misdemeanours" of her husband's libido? Chapter 2 of this book discusses at length the claim that men are significantly more promiscuous than women, and some men I describe in Chapter 5 have a tendency so strong that it's biologically and psychologically impossible for them to stop themselves from exercising their insatiable appetite. Sounds quite misogynistic from a feminist perspective, but does reality ever care about our feelings? It is what it is, and the alternative will usually be straying from a righteous path to one that is not. Again, addressing my Muslim sisters, if your husband is such a man, it then becomes a reason to at least consider his need to fulfil his desires, albeit responsibly, which is what polygamy is. I would go further and even encourage you to recommend this noble outlet for him if you fear the ignoble and prohibited alternative will tempt him, and you know him best.

Inability To Lower His Gaze

His eyes are roaming everywhere, and the sexualisation of virtually everything around him does not help him to lower his gaze as is required according to religious teachings. Nor is he even thinking about it. His vision strays even during moments he spends with his wife and family. So what? The critic and even some advocates may ridicule the notion as another preposterous argument for polygamy. I do not claim it is the answer; rather, the point I am trying to make to my Muslim sister is that his constantly straying eyes in your presence should be signalling a strong message to you that he is a man who has a strong attraction to the opposite sex. If that attraction is not kept under control, he could possibly stray even more egregiously than mere glances here and there.

The Surplus Of Women In The World

In many places around the world, and in particular war zones, the first casualty of conflict is usually men. No one can argue that war widows and orphans have the right to be taken care of. This is enshrined in religious as well as humanitarian law. So why don't you just help them financially? This is a question usually posed. Absolutely, you could do that, and that would be considered a charitable and righteous deed, but life is also more than just eating and drinking. Women require more, and men who can give them more should step up and do so. Wives of such men sometimes need to look at the bigger picture and make some concessions. Easy to do? Of course not, but it is no secret that in life, we are constantly faced with choices that sometimes require us to make them for the greater good. The scenario I described is one such scenario.

Her Husband Wants More Children

Many of us have a natural yearning for children. However, some are unable to bear a child for a number of reasons, and for others, it may take many attempts over several years. Whatever the reasons that prevent conception, as Muslims, we believe that it is God who decrees such matters. We also trust that there is a hidden wisdom behind His decree and do not know what He may be protecting us from because of it. Children come with challenges and trials, too. So that trust will bring about contentment in His decree. Anyway, enough of the philosophy.

Although it is a very hard and heartbreaking thing to do, a wife may want to consider accepting polygamy for her husband to fulfil his yearning for a child. This would be a magnanimous gesture from his wife and something he should never take for granted. He, on the other hand, should gauge the situation and his wife's delicate emotions carefully, weighing the pros and cons and taking a well-thought-out and sensitive decision thereafter.

Free Time And Space For Herself

Like many different types of relationships and arrangements where there are periods of intense activity and periods of lull, marriage is the same. As the relationship advances and matures, the needs of each party change and evolve. Whereas, at the beginning of a marriage, couples are usually inseparable and cannot get enough of each other, this is not always the case after a few years. Children happen, work commitments increase, and a routine sets in, rendering the relationship somewhat lacklustre and missing the spark that lit up the early stages of their marriage.

The cynic, predicting where I am heading with this, will be like, "This guy can't be serious?" Sorry to disappoint, but I am. From personal experience and the experience of other men, by its very nature and because of the way it is practised, polygamy has the possibility to rejuvenate the relationship between a husband and his first wife. It is commonly said that absence makes the heart grow fonder, and personally, I found this to be true. Wives who do find themselves in a polygamous arrangement and have accepted their destiny encounter two situations that they come to realise are surprisingly pleasant. Free time and space to do what she likes without the demands that come with being a wife; and a sense of eagerness to greet her man after a day or two of his absence. The spark, if it did leave, will come back in all its glory.

Takeaway

The main takeaway from this section, which is primarily addressed to Muslims, and particularly Muslim women, is to acknowledge that polygamy is definitely a concession that you make when you do not necessarily have to. The magnanimity of your actions would bring some heartbreak even if your husband traversed this path in the noblest of ways, taking into consideration your feelings at every juncture of his journey. But what it will also do is elevate you to a spiritual rank that many can never reach, and In Sha Allah, you will receive a reward many can only dream about. It will also endear you to those near and far who have witnessed or heard how stoic and respectable you behaved through this "ordeal". May God bless you abundantly for your sacrifices. Amen.

CHAPTER 10

The Husband: The Polygamist

To the men who wish to undertake this journey, did you think that I had forgotten about you? You got this far into the book, so obviously you know I didn't. It's been largely about you and how you have positioned yourself in different ways to undertake this journey to essentially satisfy your physical desires and lust. You have traversed this journey in a way that is noble (I hope) but have left a lot of emotional "debris" behind, affecting those close to you.

By now, you must have learned and understood that the journey to polygamy and the journey within polygamy is certainly not a walk in the park that seamlessly provides you the opportunity to enjoy that 'half hour of extra entertainment' each night. There is much physical and emotional effort that is required of you to make it work well, all with the goal of your happiness and contentment in mind. Remember, your contentment can never be complete unless those around you and affected by your actions are also content. This chapter is dedicated to you.

Emotional Turmoil & Mental Health

Few people will believe that this journey you chose to make with no gun pointed at your head exacts a level of stress so heavy that it can be detrimental to your mental health. And, except for your mother – maybe – fewer people will care, particularly if they are not convinced that polygamy was the only natural outlet for you. How could it be when they are convinced you are gleefully entertaining yourself and enjoying the company of another woman while your first wife has had her heart broken? Scumbag and pervert are some adjectives heading your way, either by words or thoughts.

Some men may possibly have had it easier than others, and the mental strain would naturally have been less, but there is always some level of strain and stress you experience during the journey. For example, stress from contemplating how your first wife and family have been affected and how they will treat you henceforth; stress from thinking about how you will manage your finances equitably; stress from navigating and managing the different personalities of your new wife and meeting her needs. Subsidiary stress can come from other relatives and friends close to your respective families who want to see that you are treating them right. Stress from unexpected places will surface uninvited, threatening to break your resolve and affecting your mental well-being. It is real, and it needs to be dealt with. So how?

Stress relief techniques are many, and there are several ways for you to find a semblance of calm, if not solutions, to remove them completely. Play a sport that you enjoy, find a hobby that occupies your mind, or if you can, take a short spiritual hiatus on your own, away from everyone and everything contributing to your stress. Personally, I believe that if the strain is bringing you down and making you almost dysfunctional in the environment you are in, then talking to someone uninhibitedly can be a rewarding outlet to express your feelings. That person you wish to talk to should be either a professional counsellor or another man who has gone through a similar polygamous experience. He will share his experience and insights, which will open the door of solace for you, and he will also offer you pragmatic solutions to deal with the stress. But avoid bottling it up. If that doesn't work, you could read my book again. No, I'm serious.

Whichever way you decide to help yourself, please do so unashamedly and do not neglect your mental health. You have responsibilities now, and you need to be fully fit, physically and mentally, to take them on.

Biting Off More Than You Can Chew

The phrase 'biting off more than you can chew' has obviously nothing to do with food. For those who are unfamiliar with this phrase, it means taking on more work or a bigger task than one can handle. If you have not figured it out by now, searching for, finding, and then eventually marrying a second woman involves a huge amount of work and a task many men simply do not have the fortitude to undertake. Some men know this and wisely and happily stick to their own missus, even though, in fantasy land, they would love to taste the sweetness that variety brings. I got in trouble for saying what I just said, but I did promise that political incorrectness and unfiltered expressions would be the hallmark of my book. Facts, as I have said before, do not care about feelings.

Wisdom, however, may not be a forte for many of you who wish to pursue this path to satisfy your desires. You are only thinking about that 'half hour of extra entertainment'. Nothing fundamentally wrong with that, but please allow yourself the chance for a breather to contemplate, and then realise that twenty-four hours minus thirty minutes leaves you with twenty-three plus hours. How are you going to deal with the remaining time?

So here I list some practical ways you could possibly 'bite off more than you can chew' in the polygamy equation.

• *Financial Constraints*

I have stressed this point before, but it is worth reiterating. Before you even think about the idea of marrying again, enrol yourself in a financial budgeting master course. I am not joking. You cannot afford to miscalculate your finances and then offer false promises, particularly to the new wife or wife-to-be whom you are obliged to support. Many women are simple people with simple needs and not demanding, but many are unforgiving. The inevitable conflict will probably cross over to and inconvenience your first wife and family, and potentially to anyone else you are responsible for because you made commitments to all of them but now find yourself in a financial hole. If you are unable to manage your finances across two families, give up the idea, and yes – you guessed it right – take up voluntary fasting.

Alternatively, you could try to find someone who would be agreeable to what is referred to as a Misyaar marriage, which I discuss in a separate section in this chapter.

• Physical Constraints

Physical constraints can fall under two headings. Let's deal with the less embarrassing one first. Polygamy obligates upon you the requirement to be equal with your wives in terms of the part of your time afforded to them, and it also requires you to provide each wife separate accommodation. What this means is that, at the very least, you will have to physically journey each day to your wives' homes and spend almost the same amount of time with each of them. If they live in the same apartment building or complex, the chore is made easier. However, if they live in different localities, different cities, or even different countries, it becomes progressively complicated and exponentially more expensive. You may have to solicit one of your wives' – most likely your second – permission to exonerate you from the strict adherence to equal time if the physical journey is tedious and frankly not possible. Of course, she has the option to accept or reject your request and you are in no position to demand from her what she has the God-given right to. So, figure it all out before you embark on this path.

The more embarrassing physical constraint is when a man does not have the ability to fulfil the rights of both his wives where intimacy is concerned. For whatever reason, be it biological or psychological. I struggle to understand who in their right mind would venture into the world of polygamy if he knows he is unable to meet the most fundamental needs that come with marriage. Perhaps he is acutely unaware and finds out the hard way after it is too late. He will need to treat himself with enhancement drugs or their like, and quickly.

• Emotional Constraints

What constitutes emotional constraints? This is the idea that a man cannot mentally give his all to his second wife because he is carrying some emotional baggage with him from his first marriage. This can happen when the excitement of that 'half hour of extra entertainment' wears off, and the man then comes to terms with his newly married life after the initial joy of intimacy. He realises at that point he was really only after one thing and that the emotional requirements of his new wife can't be met. He has the comfort of emotional security that he is accustomed to in his first wife but is unable to replicate the same feelings with his new bride. This now becomes a disaster for the unsuspecting lady whom he married because she was made to understand that he was genuine towards her. He may have actually believed he was, but he miscalculated his emotions and basically messed up someone's life and his own reputation. Unforgivable really, but redeemable if he opens his heart to embracing this new situation and looks for the good in his new wife. The point is he must try his best to find a spark to continue what he started because someone else's life is being suspended on account of his careless and callous 'one-track-mind' approach.

As we have previously said, no circumstance is identical, and there are possibilities where emotional comfort can be derived from the marriage to a second woman. This can happen if the first marriage is not a completely happy or fulfilling one, but for a variety of reasons, the marriage continues, and the couple resigns themselves to the lacklustre status quo. Not an easy situation to deal with, particularly for the first wife and even more so where children are involved. Perhaps divorce is the most pragmatic solution, which allows her the opportunity to find a new life that will be fulfilling. Yes, you would be back to square one with only one wife, but then again, in this particular situation, you didn't marry a second one with a polygamous intent behind it, did you?

Serial Polygamy

Serial polygamy is a phrase I actually - and proudly - thought I had coined myself until I discovered that good old Dr Google beat me to it, albeit his definition – which didn't really make too much sense to me – is actually not my definition. So, what is my definition of Serial Polygamy? It is the practice where a married man finds himself, consciously or unconsciously, entering into and leaving, by way of a divorce, a legitimate marriage sanctioned under the law, on multiple occasions and frequently within relatively short periods of time. That **was** a mouthful! In the case of Muslim men, it is Islamic law I am referring to; however, it could be any law acknowledged under any jurisdiction that sanctions the matrimonial union of a man and a woman.

So, is it a good thing, or is it bad? Or should we be ambivalent about it? My view is that it should never be looked at favourably and normalised in society, especially in the context of the modern era, where divorce rates are skyrocketing to unprecedented levels. Divorce is never considered a good thing insofar as it affects families and communities detrimentally more than it does beneficially unless, of course, the marriage was a very toxic one. So, to adopt such a wayward lifestyle consciously and deliberately is, at best, irresponsible and, at worst, sinister. It is displaying an insincerity towards God, your family, and the woman whom you want to make your second wife.

It can happen unconsciously, too, in your pursuit to find the right person, and while you do have sincere intentions without a sinister agenda, circumstances dictate that your several attempts to find the "right one" fall flat on your face. There are only so many instances of you getting it wrong, albeit inadvertently, after which you need to have a reality check. Do so by investing in a full-size mirror, fixing it on your wall, standing in front of it, addressing the "idiot" you see in the reflection and admonishing him by insisting and saying, "Buddy, this is not for you!" I'm serious here, although a bathroom mirror would also do the trick. I dare say you are another candidate for voluntary fasting.

Temporary Marriages

Not exactly the same thing as serial polygamy, but it's closely linked to it in terms of deception and insincerity. In such a scenario, however, the guilty parties are both the man and his "wife" unless the lady in question is completely unaware that she has agreed to such terms. So, what constitutes temporary marriage? It is one where, in the contract of marriage between both parties, it is stipulated that the marriage will last for a specified period of time, be it hours, days, weeks, months, or years. Muslims should know that such an arrangement is specifically prohibited by Islam and, therefore, considered a sin. Entering into such an arrangement is no different than committing fornication or adultery, and I have mentioned how egregious such a relationship is from the Islamic perspective. So, if you have even an infinitesimal inclination to undertake such a vile arrangement, stop yourself before you wreck yourself and, by extension, those close to you.

Misyaar Marriages

Under Islamic law, a sanctioned marriage is one where certain conditions (referred to as "Pillars" of the marriage contract) are met. When these conditions have been satisfied, the marriage is considered valid, and if even one such pillar has not been fulfilled, the marriage is rejected as invalid. A valid marriage dictates that certain obligations are placed with, and rights are afforded to each spouse. These are divinely imposed obligations and God-given rights, which are non-negotiable.

However, it has been left to each of the individual spouses to either insist that their opposite half fulfil his or her respective obligations and responsibilities as part of the marriage deal or, alternatively, offer them a concession by exonerating each other of some or all of what they are responsible for. So, for example, a wife has the right to insist her husband fulfil his financial responsibilities towards her, or she can give some or all of it up **voluntarily**. This is key because exoneration that is coerced will render the spouse responsible for fulfilling his or her obligations, sinful, and rendering moot the fundamental mission of the polygamy path, which is to stay away from sin in all its different manifestations.

This is basically what constitutes Misyaar marriages, and admittedly, it comes with some controversy, largely because it is exploited by many unscrupulous Muslim men but also because it is misunderstood. Islamic academia and scholarship dispute its validity from both a legal jurisprudential perspective as well as a moral one, arguing that the spirit of the marriage union is compromised by such an arrangement. On the other hand, a number argue for its permissibility on the grounds that as long as the pillars of the marriage contract are firmly in place, what each spouse decides to insist on or exonerate each other from their respective rights is purely up to them. Personally, the latter position makes more sense to me; however, I do not impose my views and conclusions on anyone else.

For those of you who wish to tread this path, particularly if some of the constraints – financial and time – pose difficulty for you, I advise you of two things. Firstly, study the issue from the Islamic perspective thoroughly and objectively, and come to your own independent conclusion as to whether this Misyaar arrangement is permissible or not. All the while remembering that it should never be a fatwa-shopping exercise to conveniently accept a position that suits your desires or even your biases. You can fool anyone around you and even yourself, but you can never fool God. Secondly, if you do conclude that it is a permissible marriage, it is morally incumbent on you to be absolutely forthright and upfront with the lady you plan to marry under this arrangement. If the two of you are clear about what the stakes are and accept the arrangement without any coercion whatsoever, then **bismillah**, go ahead.

Takeaway

As a man who wishes to marry a second woman and who is opting to do so in a way that is respectable and forthright, you will face a lot of internal and external challenges on the way. Emotional, physical, and financial challenges can test your mettle as a man and as a Muslim and can be overwhelming at times. Simultaneously, the speeding train that is your mission to marry a second wife is unstoppable, and when it is on a head-on collision course with these challenges, there is a grave danger it can be derailed from its track. At that point, you are faced with options to perch yourself back on that track, continuing to pursue the path in a noble and dignified way, which takes a lot of willpower and gumption, or choose a path that is reckless where the consequent trajectory will probably lead to a train wreck, metaphorically speaking. Choose wisely.

CHAPTER 11

What Next?

When the dust has settled, and I mean really settled, you are now living the life that you wanted to when you first thought about the possibility. You have two wives; your family life is different, although you have established a routine, and you are getting that 'half hour of extra entertainment', transforming your mid-life crisis to a near youthful exuberance.

The initial fizz has, however, diminished because you have now come to the realisation that your journey to this point had been an uphill climb with several challenges on the way. And being the mature man that you are, realise that what happens next will also come with its own set of challenges. Challenges that may or may not be as arduous as those you faced leading up to your second marriage, yet challenges, nevertheless.

Let's talk about some of the situations that you will encounter, the unique challenges accompanying them and how to navigate them with some panache. Some may appear mundane and inconsequential, but when it's about pitting two important people in your life against each other, nothing is mundane and inconsequential.

The First Year & Teething Problems

I personally believe that the first year of marriage to a second woman is the make-or-break year. The teething problems or marital bumps that you encounter this year are not insignificant and can sometimes entice you to turn a small bump on the road into an insurmountable mountain. It's not really a big deal, but you can make it one. And sometimes, she makes it one. Why does this happen, and how can you control your sentiments?

No matter how careful you were in the search for a new wife and how thorough you thought you were in the build-up to the marriage, you never really know a person well until you live with her. Of course, the same applies from your new wife's perspective. As that happens and you spend a little time in the closed confines of your home, you may inadvertently allow yourself to perceive unfamiliarity in her persona or in your new situation as something menacing to your psyche. You must push this negativity away because it is usually bordering on hysteria and is unhealthy. Force yourself to embrace the notion that the new scenario and person you are facing is different but not necessarily threatening. When you realise this, your mind will function calmly and collectedly, and your actions and behaviour will follow suit.

So, realise a bump on the road is only a bump, and all it requires of you is to slow down and navigate carefully but swiftly around it. The road inevitably smooths off for a distance until the next bump. Repeat this in the first year a few times, and then, you will find yourself - as rock band AC/DC used to sing- 'living easy, living free, with a season ticket on a one-way ride' onto the highway of bliss en route to your destination of contentment. A little corny, I know, but it's true.

Continuity & Consistency

Once the first year has passed, you would have settled into your new lifestyle, hopefully well, and what was the 'new normal' a short while ago is now just the 'normal'. You have done well to reach this point, and your grey and thinning hair is testimony to your efforts. Navigating this stage is less complicated and should be enjoyable, and if your wives are civil to each other or even friends, there's nothing sweeter. In fact, a spring in your step will be noticed by your friends and colleagues who will ask you about it. You can even answer them with a big smile on your face, "Because I am a happy man with two wives, who are actually civil with each other." It's a proud moment, and you will be experiencing good times in general.

It didn't feel that way at the time you told your first wife of your plans, did it? I promised you that the dust would settle, and now you are experiencing the calm after that long storm. To sustain that momentum and keep the same smooth trajectory, it's vitally important you are consistent in your routine and persistent in meeting your obligations. It will not go unnoticed by those relevant to you, and you will be appreciated as the real man that you are. A hero to some and looked up to by many.

Once you have established a basic sustainable model for the lifestyle with your two families and they are satisfied with the outcome, they will naturally expect you to consistently perform your duties at the same levels. It is important, therefore, that you continue to meet their expectations and keep that momentum. They will forgive you for the occasional slip-up but will not be so forgiving if they observe an unhealthy and repeated pattern of negligence. Beware of sluggishness or lethargy creeping into your psyche and keep churning out the high-performance levels that brought you the contentment you are currently experiencing.

Holidays & Festivals

The organisation of holidays and festivals may appear to be somewhat of a mundane matter to sweat over but trust me, it has its sticking points when you are faced with juggling between two families who want to spend their time with you during these important occasions. This will happen on a few occasions every year. Wisdom is required to handle a potentially volatile situation, and your time management skills will be tested to the hilt.

Festivals are easier to navigate than holidays – or one would think – but that would depend on the proximity of each household and your ability to shuttle between them. Consider half your time in each household, and if you have the ability, buy expensive gifts for all family members. That helps to quell their disappointment of your partial absence on this very important family occasion. Or you could appeal to both wives to celebrate the day of the festival as a "one big happy family" day. Still do buy expensive gifts for everyone because you are asking members of your family to deviate to some degree from what they have been accustomed to in order to accommodate your new lifestyle. Tough life? Poor you, it's what you wanted, right?

Holidays are another challenge for you financially and time-wise because of the need for equality between wives. Taking one wife for rest, relaxation, and recreation to the beautiful Maldives Islands for three weeks and the other for an intrepid adventure to the mosquito and leach-ridden rain forests in Malaysia for four days would probably not be a good idea; nor would you be fulfilling the condition of equality. So, use the wisdom you must have gained by this time of your journey to strategize how effectively you plan to manage these times and ensure that the "happy wife-happy life" mantra is sustained. In your case, it would be "wives".

Balancing Professional & Personal Life

Many men have a hard time balancing their professional and personal lives after marriage. If you are someone like that, then you will know that the pressures of work come with a lot of challenges and can occupy much of your time and energy. So much so that after a hard day at the office, you are only looking to lay yourself on a bed, and that too for sleep only. Now, take this high-pressure scenario and multiply it by two when you marry again. It can reach highly stressful levels, but of course you knew this before embarking on this path, right?

Related to this is the need to have your own personal space that we all enjoy from time to time. Time with the boys watching the game and having a couple of non-alcoholic beers to unwind is something to look forward to, but it is something you will unfortunately not have many opportunities for while you are in a monogamous, let alone a polygamous relationship. Time management is imperative, and I briefly discuss this aspect in this section.

Dealing With Difficult Times

Every marriage and every family experience troubling times in their lives. This is an inescapable reality, and, in your case, it's a reality multiplied by two – or three or four, and if you do have four wives, at this very moment, you are probably thanking God He stopped at this number.

A death in a family is a sad and melancholy time requiring an overload of empathy, compassion, and consideration for the wife most affected by the loss. During these times, you may need to spend more time with her, and your other wife will understand because you will do the same if it was her personal loss. However, the extra time spent is required to be repaid according to Islamic law, and you should keep proper tabs on how long you were away from any wife so you can give it back to her. If she does exonerate you from this "debt", that would be due to her kindness and compassion for the situation, although she is not compelled to and is not blameworthy if she didn't. Sickness is another time which requires some slick manoeuvring because it also falls outside the daily routine that you have built and established in the lifestyle. Again, equality is key, and how you treat each wife during times of sickness is significant and very noticeable if you falter.

What happens when you fall sick? It is natural at such times to want to stay with your first wife, whom you are accustomed to and who is perhaps better equipped and more knowledgeable in dealing with your ailments. The desire to want to be with her may or may not go down well with your other wife, and even in your unwell state, you must consider her feelings. Best you trust that your second wife is capable of nursing you and allow her the opportunity to do so. If she needs to talk to your first wife about anything specific, let her do so. Hopefully, they will be civil to each other and understand that your recovery and well-being should be prioritised over any petty rivalry, if any.

Time Management

Some people have no sense of time management whatsoever. Some do. If you do, then the task of managing your time is going to be much easier as you navigate this lifestyle and all the obligations requiring your physical presence that come with it. If you have poor time management skills, find a way to quickly improve them because it will become a very critical component in successfully dealing with being in a relationship of this nature. Not to mention your work obligations and time for other family members and friends and, of course, rest, which cannot be ignored. Unfortunately, the day does not comprise of 48 hours, so you need to figure out how to organise yourself with the time you do have. It's not rocket science; however, it begins with planning your daily routine meticulously and enacting your plans steadfastly each and every day.

Divorce

A word not many people enjoy reading and fewer people will ever want to experience, yet a word that may regrettably materialize into reality at some point in the married life of many couples. In a polygamous relationship, where we have spoken in depth about how to navigate the intricacies of such a lifestyle, you may have to deal with divorce if the situation for any of the parties involved in your relationship –

including yourself – becomes unbearable for a variety of different reasons. Some of these reasons we have attempted to pre-empt in this book, and hopefully, the guidelines found here will extinguish any scent of oncoming turbulence. However, feelings and emotions are what they are, and nothing in life is foolproof. In the extremely unfortunate event that divorce – to either wife – may be on the horizon, it needs to be handled with dignity and decorum that allows each party to relinquish their respective roles with minimum trauma. Without a doubt, if the divorce takes place with your first wife, with whom your relationship may have been built over many years, there is an added dimension of melancholy that needs to be dealt with. Take it upon yourself to ensure that justice and fairness prevail for all parties concerned at every stage of this heartbreaking process of separation (through judicial means if required) so that when everything is done and dusted, the affected spouses can move on in life with dignity and self-respect. You may have to squash your ego and eat humble pie at times but believe that in the long run, this will help to lighten the heartbreak and trauma that comes with the experience and help you and your now ex tread a new path without too much emotional debris hindering your respective progress. It was destined to be, and now show your character by praying for something or someone better to replace what you and she lost.

Takeaway

The main takeaway from this section is to find a formula for sustaining a peaceful and tranquil life post-polygamy. You will find yourself confronted with new challenges, and you may not always know how to deal with them. When you do, you may find yourself miscalculating your responses, thereby taking two steps backwards. During the teething phases, pay close attention to the bumps on the way and learn how to navigate them for future reference. Maintain steadfastness thereafter and ensure you are consistent in attending to your families' socio-economic needs fairly. If you find yourself in a situation where the relationship(s) can no longer be sustained organically, take measures to end the emotional suffering as soon as possible so that life can continue for all parties concerned in a different and, hopefully, happier trajectory.

CHAPTER 12

Miscellaneous Issues

Polygamy, for me has been a profoundly intriguing journey with some memorable experiences and lifelong lessons. If you have not had these experiences or even encountered anyone who has, for good or for bad, understanding what it takes and what each affected party goes through is difficult, if not impossible.

In this book, I have attempted to take you on a journey from the inception of the idea, rationalising the philosophy behind it, to the practice of the institution based on real-life experiences. On the way, I have highlighted a number of themes, talking points and concerns that I believe must be strategically and sensitively confronted to make this journey as smooth as it possibly can be. A tall order when dealing with such an emotive topic affecting the emotions and sensibilities of those around you, but imperative for its success, or even partial success.

In this chapter, I want to touch on other miscellaneous talking points that are not irrelevant to the lifestyle.

It's Not For Everyone

While we discussed emphatically how men are obsessed with women and how polygamy is the natural and most dignified outlet to cater to that obsession, we recognize that it is not absolutely universal. There are men who do not have such strong desires, and if they are married, they are more than satisfied with their one wife, not even thinking about adding another one. They may not envy other men or dream of having such a lifestyle. And if they do, it is usually a short mental glimpse of what it could be like, after which they quickly snap out of it and continue where they left off. Your wife may ask you the question; "Why can't you be like that?" Personally, I don't recommend she look at it this way. These are the cards they have been dealt with in life, and life comes with various tests that she can and will conquer stoically. Harbouring on the "if only" in life is not productive or conducive to mental well-being.

Marrying Much Younger Women

A female relative of mine, while discussing some of the talking points connected to polygamy, said that older men only want to marry younger women. This is not exactly true, but even if it was, what exactly is wrong with that? The impression given is that these are dirty old men abandoning their first wives for someone more beautiful and sexier. It's possible, but again, the same question I ask is, "What's wrong with this? Why are they considered 'dirty old men', and how are they abandoning their first wives?" My relative didn't have a response.

The fact is it is not unnatural for older men to want to marry younger women, and it is not totally unnatural or uncommon for younger women to want to establish a relationship with an older, mature man. They are more inclined towards such men for reasons related to financial and emotional stability. The important issue here, which we have stressed again and again, is for men to be responsible and sensitive and undertake their obligations with justice and fair treatment to all those affected. Particularly, sensitivities of his first wife in a society where everyone and their dogs will have an opinion on the scandal that unfolds because her "competition" is younger and more vibrant, as they perceive it.

The main advice I would offer men who search for younger women to be their second wives is to find someone on the same intellectual wavelength, even if the age gap is a generational one. You don't want to be a babysitter, nor do you have the time or energy for teenage tantrums. Other than that, enjoy your trophy.

Marrying Older Women

The idea of marrying an older woman as your second wife is an interesting prospect. Fundamentally, of course there is absolutely nothing wrong in doing so. If you believe there is sufficient physical and intellectual chemistry between the two of you to develop and sustain the relationship for the long term, then wonderful – go for it. The effect on your first wife will likely be less dramatic because she will not feel like she is competing with someone in terms of beauty and vibrancy. The chances of your wives being friends are also higher, but then a lot depends on the factors that led to your second marriage and not every circumstance is identical.

One thing you can be sure of is that you will never be accused of "cradle-snatching", a derogatory charge that sometimes accompanies marriage to a much younger woman. You will also have the luxury of engaging with a mature personality who, more likely than not, has seen and experienced more than you have in life. These can be positives, depending on your personality and how you view the gap. Curb your ego – if it is oversized – and embrace her maturity, as she will be able to teach you a thing or two, the benefits of which can even filter down to your first marriage. If the gap is a generational one, you may encounter a few stumbling blocks in the effort to connect with each other at an emotional or psychological level. As long as these stumbling blocks are not issues that compromise your core values, they should be mere 'bumps' on the road that can be overcome with a little patience and understanding. Golden rule: Don't make a mountain out of a molehill.

Marrying Widows And Destitute Women

Marrying a woman who is in need owing to unfortunate events that have befallen her can be a selfless act if your intention is to lift someone from a destitute situation to one of relative stability. If she happens to meet the set of criteria for the second wife profile you are looking for, the upside is twofold – the noble act of genuinely helping another human being, coupled with the benefit of having someone with good chemistry who you can connect seamlessly with at a physical and emotional level.

However, remember that your objective – as part of your mission to traverse a responsible and dignified path – should be the sustainability of the relationship. You may face challenges in achieving that if the chemistry with her is not up to your mark, notwithstanding the nobility of your intentions in the first place. Before you enter into such a relationship, think about ways in which you believe you can develop and sustain it, and usually, you will know if you have it in you or not pretty quickly. If you conclude that you don't, then don't commit or enter into the relationship to only devastate her life later on. Help her find another man who can commit, or if you have the means, support her in her destitute state.

Your first wife should be less objectionable in such a scenario insofar as she believes you are entering this relationship for noble goals and not just to satisfy your desires. You don't need to ruin that belief by informing her otherwise.

Humour And Polygamy Within The Family

Humour within the family can cultivate a very laid-back and happy atmosphere, generally allowing each member to be themselves without any pretensions. Wisdom, of course, dictates that subjects they joke about and around should be tactfully chosen and not without conventional filters to recognize sensitivities that may exist among other members. Polygamy is, without a doubt, one such subject, and you will – and should – know how far you can take such a topic up the humour ladder within your own clan. If making snide and sarcastic quips provokes no tension and indeed creates a light-hearted aura in instances of a seemingly deadpan ambience in your home, by all means, crack a joke. If, however, you know that attempting witty remarks around this subject will provoke sensitivities and resentment, don't. Meet your close friends, exchange all the locker room talk you want and leave it there.

Who Sits In The Front Seat Of Your Car?

Again, a seemingly mundane matter but can easily boil over to a minor (or even major) domestic political crisis if not handled wisely. Among my personal experiences, I had a younger wife to my first wife, who would always show respect and courtesy to her co-wife and offer her the front seat whenever we all travelled together. Driving did not become a stress point for me and there was no need for me to keep tabs. If you drive, you will need to keep a register, mental or written, and ensure each wife has her equal turn to sit in the front seat. Most importantly ensure your register is accurate because if you forget, they won't. Do not, I repeat, do not request either of them for any concession favouring one over the other at any time. Drive headache-free and be safe.

Inheritance Matters

Inheritance is a component of Islamic law that is given much importance, not least because its improper application, after your death, can lead to animosity among family members and heirs in particular. When you marry again, you are including an additional heir in that equation, and instructions should be given to the estate manager – or close family members – to ensure the distribution after your demise is according to Islamic law. This becomes another reason to seriously avoid any clandestine marriage arrangements as best as you can.

However, if you were compelled to marry incognito, then choose a trusted – and brave – friend or two with this information and incontrovertible proof (of marriage) so that in the event of any eventuality, they will have to go through the ordeal of breaking the news to your family informing them that – guess what? – Actually, they have an additional heir to share in your estate. Obviously, you won't be there to witness what hit the fan, and hopefully, after the ordeal, your friend will forgive you and continue to supplicate for you.

Takeaway

Marrying another woman of any age, maturity or affluence and dealing with issues that inevitably come with marriage is not always a walk in the park. It is true when you have one wife and more so when you choose to include another in your life. You will confront a number of unpredictable situations and scenarios and need to find ways to navigate them with a level of aplomb to avoid imploding into an emotional rubble. Extracting yourself from the rubble is not easy, so it is best to avoid putting yourself there in the first place.

Final Thoughts & Conclusion

Let me conclude by saying I have really enjoyed writing this book, rekindling some of the memories and experiences of very interesting, intriguing, and peculiar times in my life. If you have gotten this far in the book, I am truly honoured, and I thank you from the bottom of my heart for staying the course. I promised you at the beginning a fascinating read and sincerely hope that you found it enjoyable and entertaining, as well as interesting, thought-provoking, and beneficial; if you did, I would have achieved much of what I set out to do.

To my Muslim brothers who wish to traverse the path from monogamy to polygamy, it simply cannot be repeated emphatically and often enough that you will be entering a monumentally life-changing phase in your life, in particular, your relationship with your first wife. How you conduct yourself before, during, and after the journey is complete will speak volumes about your character as a man and dictate how the rest of your married life will pan out. Pre-empting the expected and dealing with it aptly is intelligence; confronting effectively and sensitively the unexpected is wisdom. Be intelligent and wise in thinking through your actions each step of the way. I hope my book helps you in your cause.

To the believing wives and my Muslim sisters, if you had the stomach to read this book, I say to you, May Allah reward you abundantly for all the sacrifices you endured to make **your husband's dreams come true.** The best rewards are with your Lord. The journey you are on was not what you asked for nor what you wanted, yet here you are in it. I

I was warned that my book may not be welcomed or appreciated in your homes, and I understand that sentiment. I do ask for your open-mindedness in seeing that what I penned down was carefully thought out, not so much to justify polygamy as an institution – you are a believer, and you accept what God has legislated – but rather to rationalise its need in society today so men like your husband, who yearn for it, can do so with dignity. A dignity that compels him to conduct himself responsibly, ensures he fulfils his obligations fully and forces him to face the consequences of his actions courageously. If he does all this, you cannot but respect him as a real man, even if you dislike his energised libido.

To my non-Muslim readers, if any, my hope is that you found my book educational in learning some aspects of polygamy and its rationale from an Islamic perspective, as well as enlightening in understanding how it should function in Muslim societies. Some of you may find it strange, objectionable, or even misogynistic insofar as the allowance is given only to Muslim men. I lived much of my life in liberal societies, so I get it. There are plenty of Islamic scholastic resources that can help you understand this rationale, if you wish to do so further. Agree or disagree, yet I believe we can come to at least one common term and that is polygamy is certainly a sensible alternative to infidelity.

I hope that, given my experiences, I was able to articulate my thoughts, my feelings, and my rationales in an effective and positive way, making it useful for those who plan to undertake the journey and enlightening those who don't and never will. For those curious about what goes on behind the scenes of a polygamous marriage, I hope my book shed some light and satisfied your curiosity. Contrary to popular belief, curiosity didn't kill the cat, and it won't kill you.

Polygamy is veiled in mystery and, to many people, steeped with controversy. For those who are vehemently opposed to this lifestyle,

I absolutely do know where you are coming from. However, it is my fervent hope that as you have read my book, you have done so with an open mind, re-examining some of your objections and, most of all, affording yourself the opportunity to look at this practice and lifestyle from a different lens.

Finally, let me say the following to men contemplating this lifestyle. If you decide to "marry two, three or four but" believe, based on what you have read in this book, that you will be unable to do justice to yourself and those affected by your decisions, seriously reconsider pursuing this path in order that you and your precious family may live long and prosper!

Praise be to Allah, the Lord of the Universe and peace and salutations be on His Final Messenger, Muhammad.

www.ingramcontent.com/pod-product-compliance
Lightning Source LLC
Chambersburg PA
CBHW070046100426
42740CB00013B/2826